Careers
in Focus

Publishing

Ferguson Publishing Company
Chicago, Illinois

Andrew Morkes, *Managing Editor-Career Publications*
Carol Yehling, *Senior Editor*
Anne Paterson, *Editor*
Nora Walsh, *Editorial Assistant*

Copyright © 2001 Ferguson Publishing Company
ISBN 0-89434-326-2

Library of Congress Cataloging-in-Publication Data

Careers in Focus. Publishing
    p. cm.
  Includes index.
  ISBN 0-89434-326-2
      1. Book industries and trade--Vocational guidance--United States.
2. Publishers and publishing--Vocational guidance--United States.
[1. Publishers and publishing--Vocational guidance. 2. Vocational guidance.]
I. Title: Publishing.

Z471 .C38 2000
070.5'023'73--dc21
                                                              00-037647

Printed in the United States of America

Cover photo courtesy Kaluzny/Thatcher/Tony Stone Images

Published and distributed by
Ferguson Publishing Company
200 West Jackson Boulevard, 7th Floor
Chicago, Illinois 60606
800-306-9941
www.fergpubco.com

X-8

Table of Contents

Introduction

The publishing industry can be broken down into categories, according to the kinds of publications that are produced by publishers: books, periodicals, and miscellaneous publications.

Generally speaking, a book consists of pages that have been bound in some way to form a single volume. The United Nations Educational, Scientific and Cultural Organization, which needed a definition in order to collect statistical data, decided that a book is "a nonperiodical printed publication of at least 49 pages excluding covers." Although there are many kinds of books, three of the largest categories of books are textbooks, trade books, and technical and professional books.

Periodicals are publications that appear at regular intervals, such as daily, weekly, monthly, and quarterly. The two major types of periodicals are newspapers and magazines. Although they are sometimes quite similar, newspapers tend to appear more frequently and to contain more time-sensitive information than magazines. In addition, newspapers are generally printed on relatively inexpensive paper and have large, unbound pages. Magazines, however, often use better and more expensive paper stock and are stapled or bound.

Other kinds of specialty publications include greeting cards, calendars, blank books, diaries, scheduling organizers, and postcards, to name only a few.

Internet publishing is increasing at an extremely rapid rate. Magazines, books, journals, and various other publications have been designed specifically for the Internet, and in some cases the entire texts of books are available to be downloaded. Internet publishing will no doubt continue to expand. Most traditional print publishers of any size also have a Web presence. Book publishers use the Internet as a marketing tool, to promote and sell their publications.

Publishing companies usually are divided into the following departments: editorial, which prepares written material and artwork for publication; production, which turns the material into the final printed piece; marketing, which promotes the product; sales, which sells the product; and the personnel, clerical, and accounting departments, which provide the organizational and financial support required by any business. Many newspapers and some other publishers have their own printing facilities, in which case they have a prepress department, which prepares the publication for printing, and a printing department. Most publishers, however, hire printers, bookbinders, and other specialists.

Overall, the outlook for book publishing is good. According to the 1998 *U.S. Industry and Trade Outlook*, the total world consumption of printed products was approximately $750 billion in 1997. The Association of American Publishers (AAP) estimated that U.S. book sales were over $21 billion in 1997. That figure indicates an increase of 2.4 percent over 1996 sales. Textbook sales also increased significantly.

According to the 1998 *U.S. Industry and Trade Outlook*, newspapers have not done as well as book publishers in recent years. In the United States and other industrialized nations, newspapers have seen their circulation decrease. At the same time, although advertising revenues have increased slightly, newspapers' share of total advertising has slipped as television, other print media, and the Internet have increased their percentages. In developing countries, however, both circulation and advertising are on the rise. Various large U.S. publishers have expanded their overseas operations in an attempt to make themselves more commercially viable. It is expected that newspaper revenues will remain fairly static in the coming years. The trend toward local papers being bought by large chains is also expected to continue.

The magazine business is in good shape. Overall increases in circulation, which are under 10 percent per year, are not dramatic but are steady. Many magazines publishers are expanding their operations by publishing abroad, taking advantage of vital overseas markets. At the same time, publishers are focusing on the Internet. As paper has become more expensive, publishers have become more motivated to provide products that do not require expenditures on paper. The U.S. economy continues to be remarkably strong, and consumers continue to spend money on a wide variety of publications.

Each article in this book discusses a particular publishing industry occupation in detail. The information comes from Ferguson's *Encyclopedia of Careers and Vocational Guidance*. The **History** section describes the history of the particular job as it relates to the overall development of its industry or field. The **Job** describes the primary and secondary duties of the job. Requirements discusses high school and postsecondary education and training requirements, any certification or licensing necessary, and any other personal requirements for success in the job. Exploring offers suggestions on how to gain some experience in or knowledge of the particular job before making a firm educational and financial commitment. The focus is on what can be done while still in high school (or in the early years of college) to gain a better understanding of the job. The **Employers** section gives an overview of typical places of employment for the job. **Starting Out** discusses the best ways to land that first job, be it through the college placement office, newspaper ads, or personal contact. The **Advancement** section describes what kind of career path to expect from the job and how to get there. Earnings lists salary ranges and describes the typical fringe benefits. The **Work Environment** section describes the typical surroundings and conditions of employment—whether indoors or outdoors, noisy or quiet, social or independent, and so on. Also discussed are typical hours worked, any seasonal fluctuations, and the stresses and strains of the job. The **Outlook** section summarizes the job in terms of the general economy and industry projections. For the most part, Outlook information is obtained from the Bureau of Labor Statistics and is supplemented by information taken from professional associations. Job growth terms follow those used in the *Occupational Outlook Handbook*: Growth described as "much faster than the average" means an increase of 36 percent or more. Growth described as "faster than the average" means an increase of 21 to 35 percent. Growth described as "about as fast as the average" means an increase of 10 to 20 percent. Growth described as "little change or more slowly than the average" means an increase of 0 to 9 percent. "Decline" means a decrease of 1 percent or more.

Each article ends with **For More Information**, which lists organizations that can provide career information on training, education, internships, scholarships, and job placement.

Advertising Workers

	School Subjects
English	
Psychology	
	Personal Skills
Artistic	
Communication/ideas	
	Work Environment
Primarily indoors	
Primarily one location	
	Minimum Education Level
Bachelor's degree	
	Salary Range
$16,000 to $44,000 to $92,000+	
	Certification or Licensing
None available	
	Outlook
About as fast as the average	

Overview

Advertising is defined as mass communication paid for by an advertiser to persuade a particular segment of the public to adopt ideas or take actions of benefit to the advertiser. *Advertising workers* perform the various creative and business activities needed to take an advertisement from the research stage, to creative concept, through production, and finally to its intended audience. The advertising industry employs 250,000 people at over 20,000 advertising organizations in the United States, including agencies, large corporations, and service and supply houses.

History

Advertising has been around as long as people have been exchanging goods and services. While a number of innovations spurred the development of advertising, it wasn't until the invention of the printing press in the 15th century that merchants began posting handbills in order to advertise their goods and services. By the 19th century, newspapers became an important means of advertising, followed by magazines in the late 1800s.

One of the problems confronting merchants in the early days of advertising was where to place their ads to generate the most business. In response, a number of people emerged who specialized in the area of advertising, accepting ads and posting them conspicuously. These agents were the first advertising workers. As competition among merchants increased, many of these agents offered to compose ads, as well as post them, for their clients.

Today, with intense competition among both new and existing businesses, advertising has become a necessity in the marketing of goods and services alike. At the same time, the advertising worker's job has grown more demanding and complex than ever. With a wide variety of media from which advertisers can choose—including newspapers, magazines, billboards, radio, television, film and video, the World Wide Web, and a variety of other new technologies—today's advertising worker must not only develop and create ads and campaigns but keep abreast of current and developing buying and technology trends as well.

The Job

About seven out of every ten advertising organizations in the United States are full-service operations, offering their clients a broad range of services, including copywriting, graphics and other art-related work, production, media placement, and tracking and follow-up. These advertising agencies may have hundreds of people working in a dozen different departments, while smaller companies often employ just a handful of employees. Most agencies, however, have at least five departments: contact, research, media, creative, and production.

Contact department personnel are responsible for attracting new customers and maintaining relationships with existing ones. Heading the contact department, *advertising agency managers* are concerned with the overall activities of the company. They formulate plans to generate business, by either soliciting new accounts or getting additional business from established clients. In addition, they meet with department heads to coordinate their operations and to create policies and procedures.

Advertising account executives are the contact department employees responsible for maintaining good relations between their clients and the agency. Acting as liaisons, they represent the agency to its clients and must therefore be able to communicate clearly and effectively. After examining clients' advertising objectives, account executives develop campaigns or strategies and then work with others from the various agency departments to target specific audiences, create advertising communications, and execute the campaigns. Presenting concepts, as well as the ad campaign at various stages of completion, to clients for their feedback and approval, account executives must have some knowledge of overall marketing strategies and be able to sell ideas.

Working with account executives, employees in the research department gather, analyze, and interpret the information needed to make a client's advertising campaign successful. By determining who the potential buyers of a product or service will be, *researchers* predict which theme will have the most impact, what kind of packaging and price will have the most appeal, and which media will be the most effective.

Guided by a *research director,* research workers conduct local, regional, and national surveys in order to examine consumer preferences and then determine potential sales for the targeted product or service based on those preferences. Researchers also gather information about competitors' products, prices, sales, and advertising methods. To learn what the buying public prefers in a client's product over a competitor's, research workers often distribute samples and then ask the users of these samples for their opinions of the product. This information can then be used as testimonials about the product or as a means of identifying the most persuasive selling message in an ad.

Although research workers often recommend which media to use for an advertising campaign, *media planners* are the specialists who determine which print or broadcast media will be the most effective. Ultimately, they are responsible for choosing the combination of media that will reach the greatest number of potential buyers for the least amount of money, based on their clients' advertising strategies. Accordingly, planners must be familiar with the markets that each medium reaches, as well as the advantages and disadvantages of advertising in each.

Media buyers, often referred to as *space buyers* (for newspapers and magazines), or *time buyers* (for radio and television), do the actual purchasing of space and time according to a general plan formulated by the *media director.* In addition to ensuring that ads appear when and where they should, buyers negotiate costs for ad placement and maintain contact and extensive correspondence with clients and media representatives alike.

While the contact, research, and media departments handle the business side of a client's advertising campaign, the creative staff takes care of the artistic aspects. *Creative directors* oversee the activities of artists and writers and work with clients and account executives to determine the best advertising approaches, gain approval on concepts, and establish budgets and schedules.

Copywriters take the ideas submitted by creative directors and account executives and write descriptive text in the form of headlines, jingles, slogans, and other copy designed to attract the attention of potential buyers. In addition to being able to express themselves clearly and persuasively, copywriters must know what motivates people to buy. They must also be able to describe a product's features in a captivating and appealing way and be familiar with various advertising media. In large agencies, copywriters may be supervised by a copy chief.

Copywriters work closely with art directors to make sure that text and artwork create a unified, eye-catching arrangement. Planning the visual presentation of the client's message—from concept formulation to final artwork—the *art director* plays an important role in every stage of the creation of an advertising campaign. Art directors who work on filmed commercials and videos combine film techniques, music, and sound, as well as actors or animation, to communicate an advertiser's message. In publishing, art directors work with graphic designers, photographers, copywriters, and editors to develop brochures, catalogs, direct mail, and other printed pieces, all according to the advertising strategy.

Art directors must have a basic knowledge of graphics and design, computer software, printing, photography, and filmmaking. With the help of graphic artists, they decide where to place text and images, choose typefaces, and storyboard ads and videos. Several layouts are usually submitted to the client, who chooses one or asks for revisions until a layout or conceptualization sketch meets with final approval. The art director then selects an illustrator, graphic artist, photographer, or TV or video producer, and the project moves on to the production department of the agency.

Production departments in large ad agencies may be divided into print production and broadcast production divisions, each with its own managers and staff. *Production managers* and their assistants convert and reproduce written copy and artwork into printed, filmed, or tape-recorded form so that they can be presented to the public. Production employees work closely with imaging, printing, engraving, and other art reproduction firms and must be familiar with various printing processes, papers, inks, typography, still and motion picture photography, digital imaging, and other processes and materials.

In addition to the principle employees in the five major departments, advertising organizations work with a variety of staff or freelance employees who have specialized knowledge, education, and skill, including photographers, photoengravers, typographers, printers, telemarketers, product and package designers, and producers of display materials. Finally, rounding out most advertising establishments are various support employees, such as production coordinators, video editors, word processors, statisticians, accountants, administrators, secretaries, and clerks.

The work of advertising employees is fast-paced, dynamic, and ever-changing, depending on each client's strategies and budgets and the creative ideas generated by agency workers. In addition to innovative techniques, methods, media, and materials used by agency workers, new and emerging technologies are impacting the work of everyone in the advertising arena, from marketing executives to graphic designers. The Internet is undoubtedly the most revolutionary medium to hit the advertising scene. Through this worldwide, computer-based network, researchers are able to precisely target markets and clearly identify consumer needs. In addition, the Internet's Web pages provide media specialists with a powerful vehicle for advertising their clients' products and services. New technology has also been playing an important role in the creative area. Most art directors, for example, use a variety of computer software programs, and many create and oversee Web sites for their clients. Other interactive materials and vehicles, such as CD catalogs, touch-screens, multidimensional visuals, and voice-mail shopping, are changing the way today's advertising workers are doing their jobs.

Requirements

High School

The many kinds of advertising workers have varied educational and experiential backgrounds that defy a single set of qualifications. As a general rule, most advertising positions require a bachelor's degree; in some cases, however, it is not absolutely necessary. The creative department, for example, does not require a bachelor's degree for most entry-level positions. While having a college degree gives candidates a competitive edge, advertising establishments do not require them of their assistant copywriters. Similarly, TV producers and production department workers are less likely to need a college degree than those in other agency positions. Assistant art directors, however, usually must have at least a two-year degree from a design or art school.

You can prepare for a career as an advertising worker by taking a variety of courses at the high school level. General liberal arts courses, such as English, journalism, communication, economics, psychology, business, social science, and mathematics, are important for aspiring advertising employees. In addition, those interested in the creative side of the field should take such classes as art, drawing, graphic design, illustration, and art history. Finally, since computers play a vital role in the advertising field, you should become familiar with word processing and layout programs, as well as the World Wide Web.

Postsecondary Training

The American Association of Advertising Agencies notes that most agencies employing entry-level personnel prefer college graduates. Copywriters are best prepared with a college degree in English, journalism, or communications; research workers need college training in statistics, market research, and social studies; and most account executives have business or related degrees. Media positions are increasingly requiring a college degree in communications or a technology-related area. Media directors and research directors with a master's degree have a distinct advantage over those with only an undergraduate degree. Some research department heads even have doctorates.

While the requirements from agency to agency may vary somewhat, graduates of liberal arts colleges or those with majors in fields such as communications, journalism, business administration, or marketing research are preferred. Good language skills, as well as a broad liberal arts background, are necessary for advertising workers. College students interested in the field should therefore take such courses as English, writing, art, philosophy, foreign languages, social studies, sociology, psychology, economics, mathematics, statistics, advertising, and marketing. Some 900 degree-granting institutions throughout the United States offer specialized majors in advertising as part of their curriculum.

Other Requirements

In addition to the variety of educational and work experiences necessary for those aspiring to advertising careers, many personal characteristics are also important. Although advertising employees perform many tasks of their jobs independently, most interact with others as part of a team. In addition to working with other staff members, many advertising workers are responsible for initiating and maintaining client contact. They must therefore be able to get along well with people and communicate clearly.

Advertising is not a job that involves routine, and workers must be able to meet and adjust to the challenges presented by each new client and product or service. The ability to think clearly and logically is important, because commonsense approaches rather than gimmicks persuade people that something is worth buying. Advertising workers must also be creative, flexible, and imaginative in order to anticipate consumer demand and trends, to develop effective concepts, and to sell the ideas, products, and services of their clients.

Finally, with technology evolving at breakneck speed, it's vital for advertising workers to keep pace with technological advances and trends. In addition to being able to work with the most current software and hardware, employees should be familiar with the Web, as well as with other technology that is impacting—and will continue to impact—the industry.

Exploring

For those aspiring to jobs in the advertising industry, some insight can be gained by taking writing and art courses offered either in school or by private organizations. In addition to the theoretical ideas and techniques that such classes can provide, you can actually apply what you learn by working full- or part-time at local department stores or newspaper offices. Some advertising agencies or research firms also employ students to interview people or to conduct other market research. Work as an agency clerk or messenger may also be available. Participating in internships at an advertising or marketing organization is yet another way to explore the field, as well as to determine your aptitude for advertising work.

Employers

Most advertising workers are employed by advertising agencies that plan and prepare advertising material for their clients on a commission or service fee basis. However, some large companies and nearly all department stores prefer to handle their own advertising. Advertising workers in such organizations prepare advertising materials for in-house clients, such as the marketing or catalog department. They also may be involved in the planning, preparation, and production of special promotional materials, such as sales brochures, articles describing the activities of the organization, or Web sites. Some advertising workers are employed by owners of various media, including newspapers, magazines, radio and television networks, and outdoor advertising. Workers employed in these media are mainly sales representatives who sell advertising space or broadcast time to advertising agencies or companies that maintain their own advertising departments.

In addition to agencies, large companies, and department stores, advertising services and supply houses employ such advertising specialists as photographers, photoengravers, typographers, printers, product and package designers, display producers, and others who assist in the production of various advertising materials.

Of the 22,000 advertising agencies in the United States, most of the large firms are located in Chicago, Los Angeles, and New York. Employment opportunities are also available, however, at a variety of "small shops," four out of five of which employ fewer than 10 workers each. In addition, a growing number of self-employment and home-based business opportunities is resulting in a variety of industry jobs located in outlying areas rather than in big cities.

Starting Out

Although competition for advertising jobs is fierce and getting your foot in the door can be difficult, there is a variety of ways to launch a career in the field. Some large advertising agencies recruit college graduates and place them in training programs designed to acquaint beginners with all aspects of advertising work, but these opportunities are limited and highly competitive.

Instead, many graduates simply send resumes to businesses that employ entry-level advertising workers. Newspapers, radio and television stations, printers, photographers, and advertising agencies are but a few of the businesses that will hire beginners. The *Standard Directory of Advertising Agencies* lists the names and addresses of ad agencies all across the nation. You can find the directory in almost any public library.

Those who have had work experience in sales positions often enter the advertising field as account executives. High school graduates and other people without experience who want to work in advertising, however, may find it necessary to begin as clerks or assistants to research and production staff members or to copywriters.

Advancement

The career path in an advertising agency generally leads from trainee to skilled worker to division head and then to department head. It may also take employees from department to department, allowing them to gain more responsibility with each move. Opportunities abound for those with talent, leadership capability, and ambition.

Management positions require experience in all aspects of advertising, including agency work, communication with advertisers, and knowledge of various advertising media. Copywriters, account executives, and other advertising agency workers who demonstrate outstanding ability to deal with clients and supervise coworkers usually have a good chance of advancing to management positions. Other workers, however, prefer to acquire specialized skills. For them, advancement may mean more responsibility, the opportunity to perform more specialized tasks, and increased pay.

Advertising workers at various department stores, mail order houses, and other large firms that have their own advertising departments can also earn promotions. Advancement in any phase of advertising work is usually dependent on the employee's experience, training, and demonstrated skills.

Some qualified copywriters, artists, and account executives establish their own agencies or become marketing consultants. For these entrepreneurs, advancement may take the form of an increasing number of accounts and/or more prestigious clients.

Earnings

Salaries of advertising workers vary depending on the type of work, the size of the agency, its geographic location, the kind of accounts handled, and the agency's gross earnings. Salaries are also determined by a worker's education, aptitude, and experience. The wide range of jobs in advertising makes it difficult to estimate average salaries for all positions. Entry-level jobs, of course, may pay considerably less than the figures given in the following paragraphs.

In advertising agencies, chief executives can earn from $80,000 annually, upwards to $750,000, while experienced account executives average $44,000 a year or more. In the research and media departments, research directors average $61,000 annually, experienced analysts up to $51,800 per year, media directors between $46,000 and $92,400 annually, and media planners and buyers $27,500 to $32,500 per year. In the creative department, copywriters earn, on average, $56,000 per year, art directors between

$44,500 to $60,000 or more annually, and creative directors $92,000 per year. Finally, production managers make about $31,000 per year.

In other businesses and industries, individual earnings vary widely. Salaries of advertising workers are generally higher, however, at consumer product firms than at industrial product organizations because of the competition among consumer product producers. The majority of companies offer insurance benefits, a retirement plan, and other incentives and bonuses.

Work Environment

Conditions at most agencies are similar to those found in other offices throughout the country, except that employees must frequently work under great pressure to meet deadlines. While a traditional 40-hour workweek is the norm at some companies, one-third of the advertising industry's full-time employees report that they work 50 hours or more per week, including evenings and weekends. Bonuses and time off during slow periods are sometimes provided as a means of compensation for unusual workloads and hours.

Although some advertising employees, such as researchers, work independently on a great many tasks, most must function as part of a team. With frequent meetings with coworkers, clients, and media representatives alike, the work environment is usually energized, with ideas being exchanged, contracts being negotiated, and schedules being modified.

Advertising work is fast-paced and exciting. As a result, many employees often feel stressed out as they are constantly challenged to take initiative and be creative. Nevertheless, advertising workers enjoy both professional and personal satisfaction in seeing the culmination of their work communicated to sometimes millions of people.

Outlook

Employment opportunities in the advertising field are expected to increase about as fast as the average for all industries through 2008. Demand for advertising workers will grow as a result of increased production of goods and services, both in the United States and abroad. Network television, cable, radio, newspapers, the Web, and other media (particularly interactive vehicles) will offer advertising workers an increasing number of employment opportunities. Other media, such as magazines, direct mail, and event marketing, are expected to provide fewer job opportunities.

Advertising agencies will enjoy faster than average employment growth, as will industries that service ad agencies and other businesses in the advertising field, such as those that offer commercial photography, imaging, art, and graphics services.

At the two extremes, enormous "mega-agencies" and small shops employing up to only 10 workers each offer employment opportunities for people with experience, talent, flexibility, and drive. In addition, self-employment and home-based businesses are on the rise. Many nonindustrial companies, such as banks, schools, and hospitals, will also be creating advertising positions through the end of the century.

In general, openings will become available to replace workers who change positions, retire, or leave the field for other reasons. Competition for these jobs will be keen, however, because of the large number of qualified professionals in this traditionally desirable field. Opportunities will be best for the well-qualified and well-trained applicant. Employers favor those who are college graduates with experience, a high level of creativity, and strong communications skills. People who are not well qualified or prepared for agency work will find the advertising field increasingly difficult to enter. The same is also true for those who seek work in companies that service ad agencies.

For More Information

The AAF is the professional advertising association that binds the mutual interests of corporate advertisers, agencies, media companies, suppliers, and academia.

American Advertising Federation (AAF)
1101 Vermont Avenue, NW, Suite 500
Washington, DC 20005-6306
Tel: 202-898-0089
Web: http://www.aaf.org

The AAAA is the management-oriented national trade organization representing the advertising agency business.

American Association of Advertising Agencies (AAAA)
405 Lexington, 18th Floor
New York, NY 10174-1801
Tel: 212-682-2500
Web: http://www.aaaa.org/

The AMA is an international professional society of individual members with an interest in the practice, study, and teaching of marketing.

American Marketing Association (AMA)
311 South Wacker Drive, Suite 5800
Chicago, IL 60606
Tel: (800) AMA-1150 or (312) 542-9000
Web: http://ama.org

The Art Directors Club is an international, nonprofit organization for creatives in advertising, graphic design, interactive media, broadcast design, typography, packaging, environmental design, photography, illustration, and related disciplines.

Art Directors Club
250 Park Avenue South
New York, NY 10003
Tel: 212-674-0500
Web: http://www.adcny.org

The DMA is the largest trade association for individuals interested in database marketing.

Direct Marketing Association (DMA)
1120 Avenue of the Americas
New York, NY 10036-6700
Tel: 212-768-7277
Web: http://www.the-dma.org

The Graphic Artists Guild promotes and protects the economic interests of the artist/designer and is committed to improving conditions for all creators of graphic art and raising standards for the entire industry.

Graphic Artists Guild
90 Johns Street, Suite 403
New York, NY 10038-3202
Tel: 212-791-3400
Web: http://www.gag.org

Art Directors

Overview

Art directors play a key role in every stage of the creation of an advertisement or ad campaign, from formulating concepts to supervising production. Ultimately, they are responsible for planning and overseeing the presentation of clients' messages in print or on screen, that is, in books, magazines, newspapers, television commercials, posters, and packaging, as well as in film and video and on the World Wide Web.

In publishing, art directors work with artists, photographers, and text editors to develop visual images and generate copy, according to the marketing strategy. They are responsible for evaluating existing illustrations, determining presentation styles and techniques, hiring both staff and freelance talent, working with layouts, and preparing budgets.

In films, videos, and television commercials, art directors set the general look of the visual elements and approve the props, costumes, and models. In addition, they are involved in casting, editing, and selecting the music. In film (motion pictures) and video, the art director is usually an experienced animator or computer/graphic arts designer who supervises the animators.

In sum, art directors are charged with selling to, informing, and educating consumers. They supervise both in-house and off-site staff, handle executive issues, and oversee the entire artistic production process. In 1998, there were over 308,000 visual artists and art directors in the United States.

History

Artists have always been an important part of the creative process. In illustrating the first books, artists painted their subjects by hand using a technique called "illumination," which required putting egg-white tempera on vellum. Each copy of each book had to be printed and illustrated individually, often by the same person.

Printed illustrations first appeared in books in 1461. Through the years, prints were made through lithography, woodblock, and other means of duplicating images. Although making many copies of the same illustration was now possible, publishers still depended on individual artists to create the original works. Text editors usually decided what was to be illustrated and how, while artists commonly supervised the production of the artwork.

The first art directors were probably staff illustrators for book publishers. As the publishing industry grew more complex, with such new technologies as photography and film, art direction evolved into a more supervisory position and became a full-time job. Publishers and advertisers began to need specialists who could acquire and use illustrations. Women's magazines, such as *Vogue* and *Harper's Bazaar*, and photo magazines, such as *National Geographic* and *Life*, relied so much on illustration that the photo editor and art director began to carry as much power as the text editor.

With the creation of animation, art directors became more indispensable than ever. Animated short films, such as the early Mickey Mouse cartoons, were usually supervised by art directors. Walt Disney, himself, was the art director on many of his early pictures. And as full-length films have moved into animation, the sheer number of illustrations require more than one art director to oversee the project.

Today's art directors supervise almost every type of visual project produced. Through a variety of methods and media, from television and film to magazines and comic books, art directors communicate ideas by selecting and supervising every element that goes into the finished product.

The Job

Art directors are responsible for all visual aspects of printed or on-screen projects. Overseeing the process of developing visual solutions to a variety of communication problems, the art director helps to establish corporate identities; advertises products and services; enhances books, magazines, newsletters, and other publications; and creates television commercials, film and video productions, and Web sites. Some art directors with experience or knowledge in specific fields specialize in such areas as packaging, exhibitions and displays, or the Internet. But all directors, even those with specialized backgrounds, must be skilled in and knowledgeable about not only design and illustration but also photography, computers, research, and writing in order to supervise the work of graphic artists, photographers, copywriters, text editors, and other employees.

In print advertising and publishing, art directors may begin with the client's concept or develop one in collaboration with the copywriter and account executive. Once the concept is established, the next step is to decide on the most effective way to communicate it. If there is text, for example, should the art director choose illustrations based on specific text references, or should the illustrations fill in the gaps in the copy? If a piece is being revised, existing illustrations must be reevaluated.

After deciding what needs to be illustrated, art directors must find sources that can create or provide the art. Photo agencies, for example, have photos and illustrations on thousands of different subjects. If, however, the desired illustration does not exist, it may have to be commissioned or designed by one of the staff designers. Commissioning artwork means that the art director contacts a photographer or illustrator and explains what is needed. A price is settled on, and the artist creates the image specifically for the art director.

Once the illustrations have been secured, they must be presented in an appealing manner. The art director supervises (and may help in the production of) the layout of the piece and presents the final version to the client or creative director. Laying out is the process of figuring out where every image, headline, and block of text will be placed on the page. The size, style, and method of reproduction must all be specifically indicated so that the image is recreated as the director intended it.

In broadcast advertising and film and video, the art director has a wide variety of responsibilities and often interacts with an enormous number of creative professionals. Working with directors and producers, art directors interpret scripts and create or select settings in order to visually convey the story or the message. Ultimately responsible for all visual aspects of the finished product, the art director oversees and channels the talents of set decorators and designers, model makers, location managers, propmasters, construction coordinators, and special effects people. In addition, art directors work with writers, unit production managers, cinematographers, costume designers, and post-production staff, including editors and employees responsible for scoring and titles.

The process of producing a television commercial begins in much the same way that a printed advertising piece is created. The art director may start with the client's concept or create one in-house in collaboration with staff members. Once a concept has been created and the copywriter has generated the corresponding text, the art director sketches a rough storyboard based on the writer's ideas, and the plan is presented for review to the creative director. The next step is to develop a finished storyboard, with larger and more detailed frames (the individual scenes) in color. This storyboard is presented to the client for review and used as a guide for the film director as well.

Technology has been playing an increasingly important role in the art director's job. Most art directors, for example, use a variety of computer software programs, including PageMaker, QuarkXPress, CorelDRAW, FrameMaker, Adobe Illustrator, and Photoshop. Many others create and oversee Web sites for clients and work with other interactive media and materials, including CD-ROM, touch-screens, multidimensional visuals, and new animation programs.

Art directors usually work on more than one project at a time and must be able to keep numerous, unrelated details straight. They often work under pressure of a deadline and yet must remain calm and pleasant when dealing with clients and staff. Because they are supervisors, art directors are often called upon to resolve problems, not only with projects but with employees as well.

Art directors are not entry-level workers. They usually have years of experience working at lower-level jobs in the field before gaining the knowledge needed to supervise projects. Depending on whether they work primarily in publishing or film, art directors have to know how printing presses operate or how film is processed and be familiar with a variety of production techniques in order to understand the wide range of ways that images can be manipulated to meet the needs of a project.

Requirements

High School

A college degree is usually a requirement for those interested in becoming art directors; however, in some instances, it is not absolutely necessary. A variety of courses at the high school level will give students interested in pursuing a degree both a taste of college-level offerings and an idea of the skills necessary for art directors on the job. These courses include art, drawing, art history, graphic design, illustration, advertising, and desktop publishing.

In addition, math courses are important. Most of the elements of sizing an image involve calculating percentage reduction or enlargement of the original picture. This must be done with a great degree of accuracy if the overall design is going to work; for example, type size may have to be figured within one thirty second of an inch for a print project. Errors can be extremely costly and may make the project look sloppy.

Other useful courses that high school students might want to take include business, computing, English, technical drawing, cultural studies, psychology, and social science.

Postsecondary Training

According to the American Institute of Graphic Arts, 9 out of 10 artists have a college degree. Among them, 6 out of 10 have majored in graphic design, and 2 out of 10 in fine arts. In addition, almost 2 out of 10 have a master's degree. Along with general two- and four-year colleges and universities, a number of professional art schools offer two-, three-, or four-year programs with such classes as figure drawing, painting, graphic design, and other art courses, as well as classes in art history, writing, business administration, communications, and foreign languages.

Courses in advertising, marketing, photography, filmmaking, set direction, layout, desktop publishing, and fashion are also important for those interested in becoming art directors. Specialized courses, sometimes offered only at professional art schools, that may be particularly helpful for students who want to go into art direction include typography, animation, storyboard, Web-site design, and portfolio development.

Because of the rapidly increasing use of computers in design work, it is essential to have a thorough understanding of how computer art and layout programs work. In smaller companies, the art director may be responsible for operating this equipment; in larger companies, a staff person, under the direction of the art director, may use these programs. In either case, the director must know what can be done with the available equipment.

In addition to coursework at the college level, many universities and professional art schools offer graduates or students in their final year a variety of workshop projects, desktop publishing training opportunities, and internships. These programs provide students with opportunities to develop their personal design styles, as well as their portfolios.

Other Requirements

The work of an art director requires creativity, imagination, curiosity, and a sense of adventure. Art directors must be able to work with specialized materials, such as graphics, as well as make presentations on the ideas behind their work.

The ability to work well with various people and organizations is a must for art directors. They must always be up-to-date on new techniques, trends, and attitudes. And because deadlines are a constant part of the work, an ability to handle stress and pressure well is key.

Accuracy and attention to detail are important parts of the job. When the art is done correctly, the public usually pays no notice. But when a project is done badly or sloppily, many people will notice, even if they have no design training. Other requirements for art directors include time management skills and an interest in media and people's motivations and lifestyles.

Exploring

High school students can get an idea of what an art director does by working on the staff of the school newspaper, magazine, or yearbook. It may also be possible to secure a part-time job assisting the advertising director of the local newspaper or to work at an advertising agency.

Developing your own artistic talent is important, and this can be accomplished through self-training (reading books and practicing) or through courses in painting, drawing, or other creative arts. At the very least you should develop your "creative eye," that is, your ability to develop ideas visually. One way to do this is by familiarizing yourself with great works, such as paintings or highly creative magazine ads, motion pictures, videos, or commercials.

Students can also become members of a variety of advertising clubs around the nation. In addition to keeping members up-to-date on industry trends, such clubs offer job information, resources, and a variety of other benefits.

Employers

A variety of organizations in virtually all industries employs art directors. They might work at advertising agencies, publishing houses, museums, packaging firms, photography studios, marketing and public relations firms, desktop publishing outfits, service bureaus, digital pre-press houses, or printing companies. Art directors who oversee and produce on-screen products often work for film production houses, Web sites, multimedia developers, computer games developers, or television stations.

While companies of all sizes employ art directors, smaller organizations often combine the positions of graphic designer, illustrator, and art director. And although opportunities for art direction can be found all across the nation and abroad, many larger firms in such cities as Chicago, New York, and Los Angeles usually have more openings, as well as higher pay scales, than smaller companies.

Starting Out

Since an art director's job requires a great deal of experience, it is usually not considered an entry-level position. Typically, a person on a career track toward art director is hired as an assistant to an established director. Recent graduates wishing to enter advertising should have a portfolio of their work containing seven to ten sample ads to demonstrate their understanding of both the business and the media in which they want to work.

Serving as an intern is a good way to get experience and develop skills. Graduates should also consider taking an entry-level job in a publisher's art department to gain initial experience. Either way, aspiring art directors must be willing to acquire their credentials by working on various projects. This may mean working in a variety of areas, such as advertising, marketing, editing, and design.

College publications offer students a chance to gain experience and develop portfolios. In addition, many students are able to do freelance work while still in school, allowing them to make important industry contacts and gain on-the-job experience at the same time.

Advancement

While some may be content upon reaching the position of art director to remain there, many art directors take on even more responsibility within their organizations, become television directors, start their own advertising agencies, create their own Web sites, develop original multimedia programs, or launch their own magazines.

Many people who get to the position of art director do not advance beyond the title, but move on to work at more prestigious firms. Competition for positions at companies that have national reputations continues to be keen because of the sheer number of talented people interested. At smaller publications or local companies, the competition may be less intense since candidates are competing primarily against others in the local market.

Earnings

The job title of art director can mean many different things, depending on the company at which the director is employed. In general, however, art directors at advertising agencies earn about 10 percent more than their counterparts in general publishing. A beginning art director can expect to make somewhere around $30,000 per year, with some larger companies offering as much as $100,000. (Again it is important to note that these positions are not entry level; beginning art directors have probably already accumulated several years of experience in the field for which they were paid far less.)

Earnings are usually dependent upon the reputation of the art director and the size of the company. According to *Advertising Age*, agencies that made less than $3.6 million in 1997, for example, paid their art directors an average of $44,500, while agencies with gross income of $15 million to $45 million offered their directors average salaries of over $60,000. Salaries differ by region as well, with art directors in the South making an average of $45,400 and those in the West earning an average of $60,000. Most companies employing art directors offer insurance benefits, a retirement plan, and other incentives and bonuses.

Work Environment

Art directors usually work in studios or office buildings. While their work areas are ordinarily comfortable, well lit, and ventilated, they often handle glue, paint, ink, and other materials that pose safety hazards and should, therefore, exercise caution.

Art directors at art and design studios and publishing firms usually work a standard 40-hour week. Many, however, work overtime during busy periods in order to meet deadlines. Similarly, directors at film and video operations and at television studios work as many hours as required—usually many more than 40 per week—in order to finish projects according to predetermined schedules.

While art directors work independently, reviewing artwork and reading copy, much time is spent collaborating with and supervising a team of employees, often consisting of copywriters, editors, photographers, graphic artists, and account executives.

Outlook

The extent to which art director positions are in demand, like many other positions, depends on the economy in general; when times are tough, people and businesses spend less, and cutbacks are made. However, since economic conditions in the late 1990s were favorable, employment in the general area of visual art is expected to grow faster than the average through 2008. One area that shows particularly good promise for growth is the retail industry, since more and more large retail establishments—especially catalog houses—will be employing in-house advertising art directors.

In addition, producers of all kinds of products continually need advertisers to reach their potential customers, and publishers always want some type of illustrations to enhance their books and magazines. Creators of films and videos also need images in order to produce their programs, and people working with new media are increasingly looking for artists and directors to promote new and existing products and services, enhance their Web sites, develop new multimedia programs, and create multidimensional visuals.

People who can quickly and creatively generate new concepts and ideas will be in high demand.

On the other side of the coin, the supply of aspiring artists is expected to exceed the number of job openings. As a result, those wishing to enter the field will encounter keen competition, for both salaried, staff positions as well as freelance work. And although the Internet is expected to provide many opportunities for artists and art directors, some firms are hiring employees without formal art or design training to operate computer-aided design systems and oversee work.

For More Information

The AAF is the professional advertising association that binds the mutual interests of corporate advertisers, agencies, media companies, suppliers, and academia.

American Advertising Federation (AAF)
1101 Vermont Avenue, NW, Suite 500
Washington, DC 20005-6306
Tel: 202-898-0089
Web: http://www.aaf.org

The AAAA is the management-oriented national trade organization representing the advertising agency business.

American Association of Advertising Agencies (AAAA)
405 Lexington, 18th Floor
New York, NY 10174-1801
Tel: 212-682-2500
Web: http://www.aaaa.org/

The AMA is an international professional society of individual members with an interest in the practice, study, and teaching of marketing.

American Marketing Association (AMA)
311 South Wacker Drive, Suite 5800
Chicago, IL 60606
Tel: (800) AMA-1150 or (312) 542-9000
Web: http://ama.org

The Art Directors Club is an international, nonprofit organization for creatives in advertising, graphic design, interactive media, broadcast design, typography, packaging, environmental design, photography, illustration, and related disciplines.

Art Directors Club
250 Park Avenue South
New York, NY 10003
Tel: 212-674-0500
Web: http://www.adcny.org

The DMA is the largest trade association for individuals interested in database marketing.

Direct Marketing Association (DMA)
1120 Avenue of the Americas
New York, NY 10036-6700
Tel: 212-768-7277
Web: http://www.the-dma.org

The Graphic Artists Guild promotes and protects the economic interests of the artist/designer and is committed to improving conditions for all creators of graphic art and raising standards for the entire industry.

Graphic Artists Guild
90 Johns Street, Suite 403
New York, NY 10038-3202
Tel: 212-791-3400
Web: http://www.gag.org

Book Editors

Computer science English	School Subjects
Artistic Communication/ideas	Personal Skills
Primarily indoors Primarily one location	Work Environment
Bachelor's degree	Minimum Education Level
$18,000 to $25,000 to $42,500	Salary Range
None available	Certification or Licensing
Faster than the average	Outlook

Overview

Book editors acquire and prepare written material for publication in book form. Such formats include trade books (fiction and nonfiction), textbooks, and technical and professional books (which include reference books). A book editor's duties include evaluating a manuscript, accepting or rejecting it, rewriting, correcting spelling and grammar, researching, and fact checking. Book editors may work directly with printers in arranging for proofs and with artists and designers in arranging for illustration matter and determining the physical specifications of the book.

In 1998, more than 341,000 editors and writers worked for newspapers, magazines, and book publishers. Book editors are employed at small and large publishing houses, book packagers (companies that specialize in book production), associations, and government agencies. (See also *Editors*.)

The Job

The editorial department is generally the main core of any publishing house. Procedures and terminology may vary from one type of publishing house to another, but there is some general agreement among the essentials. Publishers of trade books, textbooks, and reference books all have somewhat different needs for which they have developed different editorial practices.

The editor has the principal responsibility in evaluating the manuscript. The editor responsible for seeing a book through to publication may hold any of several titles. The highest level editorial executive in a publishing house is usually the *editor-in-chief* or *editorial director*. The person holding either of these titles directs the overall operation of the editorial department. Sometimes an executive editor occupies the highest position in an editorial department. The next level of editor is often the *managing editor*, who keeps track of schedules and deadlines and must know where all manuscripts are at any given time. Other editors who handle copy include the senior editors, associate editors, assistant editors, editorial assistants, and copy editors.

In a trade-book house, the editor, usually at the senior or associate position, works with manuscripts that he or she has solicited from authors or that have been submitted by known authors or their agents. Editors who seek out authors to write manuscripts are also known as *acquisitions editors*.

In technical/professional book houses, editors commonly do more researching, revising, and rewriting than trade-book editors do. These editors are often required to be skilled in certain subjects. Editors must be sure that the subject is comprehensively covered and organized according to an agreed-upon outline. Editors contract for virtually all of the material that comes into technical/professional book houses. The authors they solicit are often scholars.

Editors who edit heavily or ask an author to revise extensively must learn to be highly diplomatic; the art of author-editor relations is a critical aspect of the editor's job.

When the editor is satisfied with the manuscript, it goes to the copy editor. The copy editor usually does the final editing of the manuscript before it goes to the typesetter. On almost any type of manuscript, the copy editor is responsible for correcting errors of spelling, punctuation, grammar, and usage.

The copy editor marks up the manuscript to indicate where different kinds of typefaces are used and where charts, illustrations, and photos may be inserted. It is important for the copy editor to discover any inconsistencies in the text and to query the author about them. The copy editor then usually acts as a liaison between the typesetter, the editor, and the author as the manuscript is typeset into galley proofs and then page proofs.

In a small house, one editor might do the work of all of the editors described here. There can also be separate fact checkers, proofreaders, style editors, also called line editors, and indexers. An assistant editor could be assigned to do many of the kinds of jobs handled by the senior or associate editors. Editorial assistants provide support for the other editors and may be required to proofread and handle some administrative duties.

Requirements

Postsecondary Training

A college degree is a requirement for entry into the field of book editing. For general editing, a degree in English or journalism is particularly valuable, although most degrees in the liberal arts are acceptable. Degrees in other fields, such as the sciences, psychology, mathematics, or applied arts, can be useful in publishing houses that produce books related to those fields. Textbook and technical/professional book houses in particular seek out editors with strengths in certain subject areas. Whatever the type of degree, the aspiring book editor needs an education with considerable emphasis on writing and communications courses.

Other Requirements

Book editors need a sharp eye for detail and a compulsion for accuracy. Intellectual curiosity, self-motivation, and a respect for deadlines are important characteristics for book editors. Knowledge of word processing and desktop publishing programs is necessary.

It goes without saying that if you are seeking a career in book editing, you not only love to read, but love books for their own sake as well. If you are not an avid reader, you are not likely to go far as a book editor. The craft and history of bookmaking itself is also something in which a young book editor should be interested. A keen interest in any subject, be it a sport, a hobby, or an avocation, can lead one into special areas of book publishing.

Employers

Book editors may find employment with small publishing houses, large publishing houses, the federal government, or book packagers, or they may be self-employed as freelancers. The major book publishers are located in larger cities, such as New York, Chicago, Los Angeles, Boston, Philadelphia, San Francisco, and Washington, DC. Publishers of professional, religious, business, and technical books are dispersed throughout the country.

Earnings

A salary survey published in *Publishers Weekly* in July of 1998 stated that editorial salaries were definitely tied to the size of the publishing company. Salaries for entry-level jobs, such as editorial assistant, range from $25,000 to $45,000. Editors in more advanced positions earn from $52,000 to $53,800 annually. The annual salary for supervisory editors ranges from $43,300 to $88,700.

Publishers usually offer employee benefits that are about average for U.S. industry. There are other benefits, however. Most editors enjoy working with people who like books, and the atmosphere of an editorial department is generally intellectual and stimulating. Some book editors have the opportunity to travel—to attend meetings, to meet with authors, or to do research.

Outlook

Most editing jobs will continue to be competitive through 2008, and employment is expected to increase faster than average, according to the *Occupational Outlook Handbook*. The growth of online publishing will increase the need for editors who are Web experts. Turnover is relatively high in publishing—editors often advance by moving to another firm or by establishing a freelance business. There are many publishers and organizations that operate with a minimal salaried staff and hire freelance editors for everything from project management to proofreading and production.

For More Information

Literary Market Place, *published annually by R. R. Bowker, lists the names of publishing companies in the United States and Canada as well as their specialties and the names of their key personnel. For additional information about careers in publishing, contact the following:*

Association of American Publishers
71 Fifth Avenue
New York, NY 10003-3004
Tel: 212-255-0200
Web: http://www.publishers.org

Florida Publishers Association (Independent Publishers)
PO Box 430
Highland City, FL 33846-0430
Tel: 941-647-5951
Web: http://www.flbookpub.org/

Cartoonists and Animators

School Subjects	
Art	
History	
Computer science	
Personal Skills	
Artistic	
Communication/ideas	
Work Environment	
Primarily indoors	
Primarily one location	
Minimum Education Level	
High school diploma	
Salary Range	
$10,400 to $78,000 to $338,000+	
Certification or Licensing	
None available	
Outlook	
Faster than the average	

Overview

Cartoonists and *animators* are illustrators who draw pictures and cartoons to amuse, educate, and persuade people.

The Job

Cartoonists draw illustrations for newspapers, books, magazines, greeting cards, movies, television shows, civic organizations, and private businesses. Cartoons most often are associated with newspaper comics or with children's television, but they are also used to highlight and interpret information in publications as well as in advertising.

Whatever their individual specialty, cartoonists and animators translate ideas onto paper or film in order to communicate these ideas to an audience. Sometimes the ideas are original; at other times they are directly related to the news of the day, to the content of a magazine article, or to a new product. After cartoonists come up with ideas, they discuss them with their employers, who include editors, producers, and creative directors at advertising agencies. Next, cartoonists sketch drawings and submit these for approval. Employers may suggest changes, which the cartoonists then make. Cartoonists use a variety of art materials, including pens, pencils, markers, crayons, paints, transparent washes, and shading sheets. They may draw on paper, acetate, or bristol board.

Animators are relying increasingly on computers in various areas of production. Computers are used to color animation art, whereas formerly, every frame was painted by hand. Computers also help animators create special effects or even entire films.

Comic strip artists tell jokes or short stories with a series of pictures. Each picture is called a frame or a panel, and each frame usually includes words as well as drawings. *Comic book artists* also tell stories with their drawings, but their stories are longer, and they are not necessarily meant to be funny.

Animators, or *motion cartoonists*, also draw individual pictures, but they must draw many more for a moving cartoon. Each picture varies only slightly from the ones before and after it in a series. When these drawings are photographed in sequence to make a film and then the film is projected at high speed, the cartoon images appear to be moving. (One can achieve a similar effect by drawing stick figures on the pages of a notepad and then flipping through the pages very quickly.) Animators today also work a great deal with computers.

Other people who work in animation are *prop designers*, who create objects used in animated films, and *layout artists*, who visualize and create the world that cartoon characters inhabit.

Editorial cartoonists comment on society by drawing pictures with messages that are usually funny, but which often have a satirical edge. Their drawings often depict famous politicians. *Portraitists* are cartoonists who specialize in drawing caricatures. Caricatures are pictures that exaggerate someone's prominent features, such as a large nose, to make them recognizable to the public. Most editorial cartoonists are also talented portraitists.

Storyboard artists work in film and television production as well as at advertising agencies. They draw cartoons or sketches that give a client an idea of what a scene or television commercial will look like before it is produced. If the director or advertising client likes the idea, the actions represented by cartoons in the storyboard will be reproduced by actors on film.

Requirements

High School

If you are interested in becoming a cartoonist or animator, you should, of course, study art in high school in addition to following a well-rounded course of study. To comment insightfully on contemporary life, it is useful to study political science, history, and social studies. English and communications classes will also help you to become a better communicator.

Postsecondary Training

Cartoonists and animators need not have a college degree, but some art training is usually expected by employers. Animators must attend art school to learn specific technical skills. Training in computers in addition to art can be especially valuable.

Other Requirements

Cartoonists and animators must be creative. In addition to having artistic talent, they must generate ideas, although it is not unusual for cartoonists to collaborate with writers for ideas. Whether they create cartoon strips or advertising campaigns, they must be able to come up with concepts and images to which the public will respond. They must have a good sense of humor and an observant eye to detect people's distinguishing characteristics and society's interesting attributes or incongruities.

Cartoonists and animators need to be flexible. Because their art is commercial, they must be willing to accommodate their employers' desires if they are to build a broad clientele and earn a decent living. They must be able to take suggestions and rejections gracefully.

Exploring

If you are interested in becoming a cartoonist or an animator, you should submit your drawings to your school paper. You also might want to draw posters to publicize activities, such as sporting events, dances, and meetings.

Scholarship assistance for art students is available from some sources. For example, the Society of Illustrators awards some 125 scholarships annually to student artists from any field. Students do not apply directly; rather, they are selected and given application materials by their instructors. The International Animated Film Society offers scholarships to high school seniors.

Employers

Employers of cartoonists and animators include editors, producers, creative directors at advertising agencies, comics syndicates, newspapers, and movie studios.

Starting Out

A few places, such as the Walt Disney studios, offer apprenticeships. To enter these programs, applicants must have attended an accredited art school for two or three years.

Formal entry-level positions for cartoonists and animators are rare, but there are several ways for artists to enter the cartooning field. Most cartoonists and animators begin by working piecemeal, selling cartoons to small publications, such as community newspapers, that buy freelance cartoons. Others assemble a portfolio of their best work and apply to publishers or the art departments of advertising agencies. In order to become established, cartoonists and animators should be willing to work for what equals less than minimum wage.

Advancement

Cartoonists' success, like that of other artists, depends upon how much the public likes their work. Very successful cartoonists and animators work for prestigious clients at the best wages; some become well known to the public.

Earnings

Freelance cartoonists may earn anywhere from $100 to $1,200 or more per drawing, but top dollar generally goes only for big, full-color projects such as magazine cover illustrations. Most cartoonists and animators average from $200 to $1,500 a week, although syndicated cartoonists on commission can earn much more. Salaries depend upon the work performed. Cel painters, as listed in a salary survey conducted by *Animation World*, start at about $750 a week; animation checkers, $930 a week; story sketchers, $1,500 weekly. According to *U.S. News & World Report*, animators, depending on their experience, can earn from $800 to $1,800 a week. Top animators can command weekly fees of about $6,500 or more. Comic strip artists are usually paid according to the number of publications that carry their strip. Self-employed artists do not receive fringe benefits such as paid vacations, sick leave, health insurance, or pension benefits.

Work Environment

Most cartoonists and animators work in big cities where employers such as television studios, magazine publishers, and advertising agencies are located. They generally work in comfortable environments, at drafting tables or drawing boards with good light. Staff cartoonists work a regular 40-hour workweek but may occasionally be expected to work evenings and weekends to meet deadlines. Freelance cartoonists have erratic schedules, and the number of hours they work may depend on how much money they want to earn or how much work they can find. They often work evenings and weekends but are not required to be at work during regular office hours.

Cartoonists and animators can be frustrated by employers who curtail their creativity, asking them to follow instructions that are contrary to what they would most like to do. Many freelance cartoonists spend a lot of time working alone at home, but cartoonists have more opportunities to interact with other people than do most working artists.

Outlook

Opportunities in this field are expected to grow faster than average through 2008, according to the U.S. Department of Labor. *U.S. News & World Report* recently included the career of animator in its list of 20 Hot Job Tracks.

Cartoons are not just for children anymore. Much of the animation today is geared for an adult audience. Interactive games, animated films, network and cable television, and the Internet are among the many employment sources for talented cartoonists and animators. Almost two-thirds of all visual artists are self-employed, but freelance work can be hard to come by and many freelancers earn little until they acquire experience and establish a good reputation. Competition for work will be keen; those with an undergraduate or advanced degree in art or film will be in demand. Experience in action drawing and computers is a must.

Animation houses, such as Disney, will continue to be good sources of jobs. The growing trend of sophisticated special effects in motion pictures will create many opportunities at industry effects houses such as Sony Pictures Image Works, DreamQuest, Industrial Light & Magic, and DreamWorks.

For More Information

For education and career information, contact:

National Cartoonists Society
Columbus Circle Station
PO Box 20267
New York, NY 10023
Tel: 212-627-1550
Web: http://www.reuben.org

For an art school directory, a scholarship guide, or general information, contact:

National Art Education Association
1916 Association Drive
Reston, VA 20191-1590
Tel: 703-860-8000
Web: http://www.naea-reston.org

For membership and scholarship information, contact:

International Animated Film Society
725 South Victory Boulevard
Burbank, CA 91502
Tel: 818-842-8330
Email: info@asifa-hollywood.org
Web: http://www.asifa-hollywood.org

For scholarship information for qualified students in art school, have your instructor contact:

Society of Illustrators
128 East 63rd Street
New York, NY 10021 7303
Email: society@societyillustrators.org
Web: http://www.societyillustrators.org

Columnists

School Subjects
English
Foreign language

Personal Skills
Communication/ideas
Helping/teaching

Work Environment
Indoors and outdoors
Primarily multiple locations

Minimum Education Level
Bachelor's degree

Salary Range
$20,000 to $40,000 to $60,000

Certification or Licensing
None available

Outlook
About as fast as the average

Overview

Columnists write opinion pieces for publication in newspapers or magazines. Some columnists work for syndicates—organizations that sell articles to many media at once.

Columnists can be generalists who write about whatever strikes them on any topic. Most columnists focus on a specialty, such as government, politics, local issues, health, humor, sports, gossip, or other themes.

Most newspapers employ local columnists or run columns from syndicates. Some syndicated columnists work out of their homes or private offices.

History

Because the earliest American newspapers were political vehicles, much of their news stories brimmed with commentary and opinion. This practice continued up until the Civil War. Horace Greeley, a popular editor who had regularly espoused partisanship in his *New York Tribune*, was the first to give editorial opinion its own page separate from the news.

As newspapers grew into instruments of mass communication, their editors sought balance and fairness on the editorial pages and began publishing a number of columns with varying viewpoints.

Famous Washington, DC-based columnist Jack Anderson is known for bringing an investigative slant to the editorial page. Art Buchwald and Molly Ivins became well known for their satirical look at government and politicians.

The growth of news and commentary on the Internet has only added to the power of columnists.

The Job

Columnists take a news story and enhance the facts with personal opinion and panache. Or a column may be based on personal experience. Either way, a column usually has a punchy start, a pithy middle, and a strong, sometimes poignant, ending.

Columnists are responsible for writing columns on a regular basis on accord with a schedule, depending on the frequency of publication. It may be that they write a column daily, weekly, quarterly, or monthly. Like other journalists, they face pressure to meet a deadline.

Most columnists are free to select their own story ideas. The need to constantly come up with new ideas may be one of the hardest parts of the job, but also one of the most rewarding. Columnists search through newspapers, magazines, and the Internet, watch television, and listen to the radio. The various types of media suggest ideas, and keep the writer aware of current events and social issues.

Next they do research, delving into a topic much like an investigative reporter would, so that they can back up their arguments with facts.

Finally, they write, usually on a computer. After a column is written, at least one editor goes over it to check for clarity and correct mistakes. Then the cycle begins again. Often a columnist will write a few relatively timeless pieces to keep for use as backups in a pinch, in case a new idea can't be found or falls through.

Most columnists work in newsrooms or magazine offices, although some, especially those who are syndicated but not affiliated with a particular newspaper, work out of their homes or private offices. Many well-known syndicated columnists work out of Washington, DC.

Newspapers often run small pictures of columnists, called head shots, next to their columns. This, and a consistent placement of a column in a particular spot in the paper, usually gives a columnist greater recognition than a reporter or editor.

Requirements

High School

High school students should take English and writing classes and participate in extracurricular activities such as the school newspaper or debate team.

Postsecondary Training

As is the case for other journalists, at least a bachelor's degree in journalism is usually required, although some journalists graduate with degrees in political science or English. Experience may be gained by writing for the college or university newspaper, and through a summer internship at a newspaper or other publication. It also may be helpful to submit freelance opinion columns to local or national publications. The more published articles, called "clips," graduates can show to prospective employers, the better.

Other Requirements

To be a columnist requires similar characteristics as those for being a reporter: curiosity, a genuine interest in people, ability to write clearly and succinctly, and the strength to thrive under deadline pressure. But columnists also require a certain wit and wisdom, the compunction to express strong opinions, and the ability to take apart an issue and debate it.

Exploring

A good way to explore this career is to work for your school newspaper and perhaps write your own column. Participation in debate clubs will help you form opinions and express them clearly.

Employers

Newspapers of all kinds run columns, as do certain magazines and even public radio stations, where a tape is played over the airways of the author reading the column. Some columnists are self-employed, preferring to market their work to syndicates instead of working for a single newspaper or magazine.

Starting Out

Most columnists start out as reporters. Experienced reporters are the ones most likely to become columnists. Occasionally, however, a relatively new reporter may suggest a weekly column if the beat being covered warrants it, for example, politics.

Another route is to start out by freelancing, sending columns out to a multitude of newspapers and magazines in the hopes that someone will pick them up. Also, columns can be marketed to syndicates. A list of these, and magazines that may also be interested in columns, is provided in the *Writer's Market*.

Advancement

Newspaper columnists can advance in national exposure by having their work syndicated. Or they may try to get a collection of their columns published in book form.

Columnists also may choose other editorial positions, such as editor, editorial writer or page editor, or foreign correspondent.

Earnings

Like reporters' salaries, the incomes of columnists vary greatly according to experience, newspaper size and location, and whether the columnist is under a union contract. But generally, columnists make higher salaries than reporters.

Average starting salaries for writers, including columnists, was about $20,000 in 1997, according to the Dow Jones Newspaper Fund. After several years of experience, columnists can make top salaries of $60,000 or more a year. According to the *Occupational Outlook Handbook*, median annual earnings for writers and editors working for periodicals were $35,900 and for newspapers, $28,500.

Freelancers may get paid by the column. Syndicates pay columnists 40 percent to 60 percent of the sales income generated by their columns or a flat fee if only one column is being sold.

Work Environment

Columnists work mostly indoors in newspaper or magazine offices, although they may occasionally conduct interviews or do research on location out of the office. Some columnists may work as much as 48 to 52 hours a week.

Outlook

The number of newspaper reporter jobs is projected to decrease in coming years, but the number of magazine writer jobs is expected to increase. Probably, like foreign correspondents, the number of columnists will remain fairly stable. If a newspaper is small, or falls on hard times, managing editors may expect a local columnist to also take on reporting duties. Competition for newspaper jobs is stiff, and for columnist positions, even stiffer, because they are highly prized among reporters and because there are so few of them. Smaller daily and weekly newspapers may be easier places to find employment than major metropolitan newspapers, and movement up the ladder to columnist will also likely be quicker, but the pay is less than at bigger papers. The increase of online publishing is expected to increase the demand for writers. The *Occupational Outlook Handbook* says employment of writers and editors is expected to increase faster than the average for all occupations through 2008.

For More Information

The ASJA provides information on careers in newspaper reporting, as well as information on education and financial aid.

American Society of Journalists and Authors (ASJA)
1501 Broadway, Suite 302
New York, NY 10036
Tel: 212-997-0947
Email: execdir@asja.org
Web: http://www.asja.org/

The AEJMC provides general educational information on all areas of journalism (newspapers, magazines, television, and radio).

**Association for Education in Journalism
and Mass Communication (AEJMC)**
121 LaConte College
University of South Carolina
Columbia, SC 29208-0251
Tel: 803-777-2006
Email: aejmc@sc.edu
Web: http://www.aejmc.sc.edu/on-line/home.html

The NAB has information on jobs, scholarships, internships, college programs, and other resources. It offers Careers in Radio ($4) *and* Careers in Television *($4), which describe the key jobs, educational requirements, and job-related experience required.*

National Association of Broadcasters (NAB)
1771 N Street, NW
Washington, DC 20036
Tel: 202-429-5300
Email: ssiroky@nab.org
Web: http://www.nab.org

The SPJ has student chapters all over the United States. Among its many services to students, it offers information on scholarships and internships.

Society of Professional Journalists (SPJ)
16 South Jackson
Greencastle, IN 46135-0077
Tel: 765-653-3333
Email: spj@spjhq.org
Web: http://www.spj.org

Desktop Publishing Specialists

	School Subjects
Art Computer science English	

	Personal Skills
Artistic Communication/ideas	

	Work Environment
Primarily one location Primarily indoors	

	Salary Range
$18,000 to $30,000 to $83,000	

	Certification or Licensing
Voluntary	

	Outlook
Much faster than the average	

Overview

Desktop publishing specialists prepare reports, brochures, books, cards, and other documents for printing. They create computer files of text, graphics, and page layout. They work with files others have created, or they compose original text and graphics for the client. There are around 26,000 desktop publishing specialists working in the printing industry, either as freelancers or for corporations, service bureaus, and advertising agencies.

History

When Johannes Gutenberg invented movable type in the 1440s, it seemed like a major technological advancement. Up until that point, books were produced entirely by hand by monks, every word written in ink on vellum. Though print shops flourished all across Europe with this invention, inspiring the production of millions of books by the 1500s, there was no other major change in the technology of printing until the 1800s. By then, cylinder presses were churning out thousands of sheets per hour, and the Linotype machine allowed for easier, more efficient plate-making. Offset lithography (a method of applying ink from a treated surface onto paper) followed and gained popularity after World War II. Phototypesetting was later developed, involving creating film images of text and pictures to be printed. At the end of the 20th century, computers caused another revolution in the industry. Laser printers now allow for low-cost, high-quality printing, and desktop publishing software is credited with spurring sales and use of personal home computers.

The Job

If you've ever used a computer to design and print flyers to promote a high school play, or if you've put together a small literary magazine, then you've had some experience in desktop publishing. Not so many years ago, the prepress process (the steps to prepare a document for the printing press) involved metal casts, molten lead, light tables, knives, wax, paste, and a number of different professionals from artists to typesetters. With computer technology, these jobs are becoming more consolidated. A desktop publishing specialist is someone with artistic talents, proofreading skills, sales and marketing abilities, and a great deal of computer knowledge. As a desktop publishing specialist, you'll work on computers converting and preparing files for printing presses and other media, such as the Internet and CD-ROM. Much of desktop publishing fits into the prepress category, and desktop publishing specialists typeset, or arrange and transform, text and graphics. Your work is performed at a home computer using the latest in design software. Macintosh programs such as FreeHand, Illustrator, and PageMaker, are the most popular with desktop publishing specialists, though PC programs like Corel Draw and PhotoShop are also gaining popularity. Some desktop publishing specialists use CAD (computer-aided design) technology, allowing them to create images and effects with a digitizing pen.

Once you've created the file to be printed, you'll either submit it to a commercial printer, or you'll print the pieces yourself. Whereas traditional typesetting costs over $20 per page, desktop printing can cost less than a penny a page. Individuals hire the services of desktop publishing specialists for creating and printing invitations, advertising and fundraising brochures, newsletters, flyers, and business cards. Commercial printing involves catalogs, brochures, and reports, while business printing encompasses products used by businesses, such as sales receipts and forms.

Typesetting and page layout work entails selecting font types and sizes, arranging column widths, checking for proper spacing between letters, words, and columns, placing graphics and pictures, and more. You'll choose from the hundreds of typefaces available, taking the purpose and tone of the text into consideration when selecting from fonts with round shapes or long shapes, thick strokes or thin, serifs or sans serifs. Editing is also an important duty of a desktop publishing specialist. Articles must be updated, or in some cases rewritten, before they are arranged on a page. As more people use their own desktop publishing programs to create print-ready files, you'll have to be skillful at designing original work, and promoting your talents, in order to remain competitive.

Darryl Gabriel and his wife Maree own a desktop publishing service in Australia—the Internet has allowed them to publicize the business globally. They currently serve customers in their local area and across Australia, and are hoping to expand more into international Internet marketing. Darryl and Maree use a computer ("But one is not enough," Darryl says), a laser printer, and a scanner to create business cards, pamphlets, labels, books, and personalized greeting cards. Though they must maintain computer skills, they also have a practical understanding of the equipment. "We keep our prices down by being able to re-ink our cartridges," Darryl says. "This takes a little getting used to at first, but once you get a knack for it, it becomes easier."

You'll be dealing with technical issues, such as resolution problems, colors that need to be corrected, and software difficulties, but you'll also use creativity and artistic skills to create designs. Many of your clients will bring you graphics they've designed themselves using computer software programs, while others will bring you drawings in pencil and paper. They provide you with their designs, and you must convert these designs to the format requested by the designers. A designer may come in with a hand-drawn sketch, a printout of a design, or a file on a diskette, and he or she may want the design to be ready for publication on the World Wide Web, in a high-quality brochure, or in a newspaper or magazine. Each format presents different issues, and you must be familiar with the processes and solutions for each. You may also provide services such as color scanning, laminating, image manipulation, and poster production.

Customer relations are as important as technical skills. Darryl emphasizes the importance of learning how to use your equipment and software to their fullest potential, but he also advises you to know your customers. "Try and be as helpful as possible to your customers," he says, "so you can provide them with products that they are happy with and that are going to benefit their businesses." He says it's also very important to follow up, calling customers to make sure they're pleased with the work. "If you're able to relate to what the customers want, and if you encourage them to be involved in the initial design process, then they'll be confident they're going to get quality products."

Requirements

High School

Classes that will help you develop desktop publishing skills include computer classes and design and art classes. Computer classes should include both hardware and software, since understanding how computers function will help you with troubleshooting and knowing the computer's limits. In photography classes you can learn about composition, color, and design elements. Typing, drafting, and print shop classes, if available, will also provide you with the opportunity to gain some indispensable skills. Working on the school newspaper or yearbook will train you on desktop publishing skills as well, including page layout, typesetting, composition, and working under a deadline.

Postsecondary Training

Although a college degree is not a prerequisite, many desktop publishing specialists have at least a bachelor's degree. Areas of study range anywhere from English and communications, to graphic design. Some two-year colleges and technical institutes offer programs in desktop publishing or related fields. A growing number of schools offer programs in technical and visual communications, which may include classes in desktop publishing, layout and design, and computer graphics. Four-year colleges also offer courses in technical communications and graphic design. There are many opportunities to take classes related to desktop publishing through extended education programs offered through universities and colleges. These classes can range from basic desktop publishing techniques to advanced courses in Adobe Photoshop or QuarkXPress and are often taught by professionals working in the industry.

A number of professional organizations and schools offer scholarship and grant opportunities. The Graphic Arts Education and Research Foundation (GAERF) and the Education Council of the Graphic Arts

Industry, Inc., both divisions of the Association for Suppliers of Printing and Publishing Technologies (NPES), can provide information on scholarship opportunities and research grants. Other organizations that offer financial awards and information on scholarship opportunities include the Society for Technical Communication, the International Prepress Association, the Printing Industries of America (PIA), and the Graphic Arts Technical Foundation, which offers scholarships in graphic communications through the National Scholarship Trust Fund.

Certification or Licensing

Certification is not mandatory, and currently there is only one certification program offered in desktop publishing. The Association of Graphic Communications has an Electronic Publishing Certificate designed to set industry standards and measure the competency levels of desktop publishing specialists. The examination is divided into a written portion and a hands-on portion. During the practical portion of the examination, candidates receive files on a disk and must manipulate images and text, make color corrections, and perform whatever tasks are necessary to create the final product. Applicants are expected to be knowledgeable in print production, color separation, typography and font management, computer hardware and software, image manipulation, page layout, scanning and color correcting, prepress and preflighting, and output device capabilities.

PIA is in the process of developing industry standards in the prepress and press industries. PIA may eventually design a certification program in desktop publishing or electronic prepress operation.

Other Requirements

Desktop publishing specialists are detail-oriented, possess problem-solving skills, and have a sense of design and artistic skills. "People tell me I have a flair for graphic design," Darryl says, "and mixing the right color with the right graphics." A good eye and patience are critical, as well as endurance to see projects through to the finish. You should have an aptitude for computers, the ability to type quickly and accurately, and a natural curiosity. A calm temperament comes in handy when working under pressure and constant deadlines. You should be flexible and be able to handle more than one project at a time.

Exploring

Experimenting with your home computer, or a computer at school or the library, will give you a good idea as to whether desktop publishing is for you. Play around with various graphic design and page layout programs. If you subscribe to an Internet service, take advantage of any free Web space available to you and design your own home page. Join computer clubs and volunteer at small organizations to produce newsletters and flyers; volunteering is an excellent way to try new software and techniques, and to gain experience troubleshooting and creating final products. Also, part-time or summer employment with printing shops and companies that have in-house publishing or printing departments are great ways to gain experience and make valuable contacts.

Employers

Your clients will include individuals and small business owners, such as publishing houses, advertising agencies, graphic design agencies, and printing shops. Some large companies also contract with desktop publishing services, rather than hire full-time staffs of designers. Government agencies hire desktop publishing specialists for the large number of documents they publish. The Government Printing Office (GPO) has a Digital Information Technology Support Group (DITS Group) that provides desktop and electronic publishing services to federal agencies.

You'll usually be dealing directly with your clients, but in some cases you may be subcontracting work from printers, designers, and other desktop publishing specialists. You may also hire your services as a consultant, working with printing professionals to help solve particular design problems.

Starting Out

To start your own business, you must have a great deal of experience with design and page layout, and a careful understanding of the computer design programs you'll be using. Before striking out on your own, you may want to gain experience as a full-time staff member of a large business. Most desktop publishing specialists enter the field through the production side, or the editorial side of the industry. Those with training as a designer or artist can easily master the finer techniques of production. Printing houses and design agencies are places to check for production artist opportunities. Publishing companies often hire desktop publishing specialists to work in-house or as freelance employees. Working within the industry, you can make connections and build up a clientele.

You can also start out by investing in computer hardware and software, and volunteering your services. By designing logos, letterhead, and restaurant menus, your work will gain quick recognition, and word of your services will spread.

Advancement

The growth of Darryl and Maree's business is requiring that they invest in another computer and printer. "We want to expand," Darryl says, "develop with technology, and venture into Internet marketing and development. We also intend to be a thorn in the side of the larger commercial printing businesses in town." In addition to taking on more print projects, you can expand your business into Web design and page layout for Internet magazines.

Earnings

There is limited salary information available for desktop publishing specialists, most likely because the job duties of desktop publishing specialists can vary and often overlap with other jobs. According to a salary survey conducted by PIA in 1997, the average wage of desktop publishing specialists in the prepress department ranged from $11.72 to $14.65 an hour, with the highest rate at $40 an hour. Entry-level desktop publishing specialists with little or no experience generally earn minimum wage. Electronic page make-up system operators earned an average of $13.62 to $16.96, and scanner operators ranged from $14.89 to $17.91.

According to the *Occupational Outlook Handbook,* full-time prepress workers in typesetting and composition earned a median wage of $443 a week, or $23,046 annually. Wage rates vary depending on experience, training, region, and size of the company.

Work Environment

Desktop publishing specialists spend most of their time working in front of a computer, whether editing text, or laying out pages. They need to be able to work with other prepress operators, and deal with clients. Hours may vary depending on project deadlines at hand. Some projects may take one day to complete, while others may take a week or longer. Projects may range from designing a logo for letterhead, preparing a catalog for the printer, or working on a file that will be published on the World Wide Web.

Outlook

According to the *Occupational Outlook Handbook*, the field of desktop publishing is projected to be one of the fastest growing occupations, increasing about 75 percent through 2008. In 1998, there were a total of 26,000 desktop publishing specialists employed in the United States. As technology advances, the ability to create and publish documents will become easier and faster, thus influencing more businesses to produce printed materials. Desktop publishing specialists will be needed to satisfy typesetting, page layout, design, and editorial demands. With new equipment, commercial printing shops will be able to shorten the turnaround time on projects and in turn can increase business and accept more jobs. For instance, digital printing presses allow printing shops to print directly to the digital press rather than printing to a piece of film, and then printing from the film to the press. Digital printing presses eliminate an entire step and should appeal to companies who need jobs completed quickly.

According to a survey conducted by PIA in 1997, the printing industry is growing, which can be attributed partly to the growth experienced by the North American economy. The electronic prepress segment of the printing market enjoyed the most growth, with an average change from 1996 of 9.3 percent. Traditional prepress, on the other hand, suffered a decline of 5.7 percent. PIA's survey also indicates that printing firms have been experiencing difficulties finding new, qualified employees. This is a good sign for desktop publishing specialists with skills and experience.

QuarkXPress, Adobe PageMaker, Macromedia FreeHand, Adobe Illustrator, and Adobe Photoshop are some programs often used in desktop publishing. Specialists with experience in these and other software will be in demand.

For More Information

For career information, and information about scholarships and education, contact:

Association for Suppliers of Printing, Publishing, and Converting Technologies
1899 Preston White Drive
Reston, VA 20191-4367
Tel: 703-264-7200
Email: npes@npes.org
Web: http://www.npes.org

For scholarship information, contact:

National Scholarship Trust Fund of the Graphic Arts
200 Deer Run Road
Sewickley, PA 15143-2600
Tel: 800-900-GATF
Email: info@gatf.org
Web: http://www.gatf.org

For career brochures and information about grants and scholarships, contact:

Society for Technical Communication
901 North Stuart Street, Suite 904
Arlington, VA 22203-1822
Tel: 703-522-4114
Web: http://www.stc-va.org

To obtain an issue of Desktop Publishers Journal, *a trade magazine for desktop publishers, contact:*

Desktop Publishers Journal
462 Boston Street
Topfield, MA 01983-1232
Tel: 978-887-7900
E-mail: edit@dtpjournal.com
Web: http://www.dtpjournal.com

Independent Computer Consultants Association
11131 South Towne Square, Suite F
St. Louis, MO 63123
Tel: 800-774-4222
Email: Web: http://www.icca.org

Editors

English Journalism	School Subjects
Communication/ideas Helping/teaching	Personal Interests
Primarily indoors Primarily one location	Work Environment
Bachelor's degree	Minimum Education Level
$21,000 to $45,000 to $67,000+	Salary Range
None available	Certification or Licensing
Faster than the average	Outlook

Overview

Editors perform a wide range of functions, but their primary responsibility is to ensure that text provided by writers is suitable in content, format, and style for the intended audiences. Readers are an editor's first priority. Among the employers of editors are book publishers, magazines, newspapers, newsletters, corporations of all kinds, advertising agencies, radio stations, television stations, and Internet sites. No accurate figures for numbers of editors employed are available, but the U.S. Department of Labor has estimated that 341,000 writers and editors were employed in 1998.

History

The history of book editing is tied closely to the history of the book and bookmaking and the history of the printing process. The 15th century invention of the printing press by German goldsmith Johannes Gutenberg and of movable type in the West revolutionized the craft of bookmaking. Books could now be mass-produced. It also became more feasible to make changes to copy before a book was put into production. Printing had been invented hundreds of years earlier in Asia, but books did not proliferate there as quickly as they did in the West, which saw millions of copies in print by 1500.

In the early days of publishing, authors worked directly with the printer, and the printer was often the publisher and seller of the author's work. Eventually, however, booksellers began to work directly with the authors and eventually took over the role of publisher. The publisher then became the middleman between author and printer.

The publisher worked closely with the author and sometimes acted as the editor; the word *editor*, in fact, derives from the Latin word *edere* or *editum* and means supervising or directing the preparation of text. Eventually, specialists were hired to perform the editing function. These editors, who were also called advisors or literary advisors in the 19th century, became an integral part of the publishing business.

The editor, also called the sponsor in some houses, sought out the best authors, worked with them, and became their advocate in the publishing house. So important did some editors become that their very presence in a publishing house could determine the quality of author that might be published there. Some author-editor collaborations have become legendary. The field has grown through the 20th century, with computers greatly speeding up the process by which editors move copy to the printer.

The Job

Editors work for many kinds of publishers, publications, and corporations. Editors' titles vary widely, not only from one area of publishing to another but also within each area.

Although some editors write for the organizations that employ them, most editors work with material provided by writers. For this reason, one of the most important steps in the editing process is acquiring the work of writers. In the fields of book and journal publishing, that work is usually performed by *acquisitions editors*, who are often called acquiring editors. Acquisitions editors may either generate their own ideas or use ideas provided by their publishers or other staff members. If they begin with an idea, they look for writers who can create an effective book or article based on that idea. One benefit of that method is that such ideas are ones that the editors believe are likely to be commercially successful or intellectually successful or both. Often, however, editors use ideas that they receive from writers in the form of proposals.

In some cases, the acquisitions editor will receive a complete manuscript from an author instead of a proposal. Most of the time, however, the writer will submit a query letter that asks whether the editor is interested in a particular idea. If the editor believes that the idea is salable and suitable for the publishing house, the editor will discuss the idea further with the writer. Unless the writer is well known or is known and trusted by the editor, the editor usually asks the writer for a sample chapter or section. If the editor likes the sample chapter and believes that the author can complete an acceptable manuscript, the publishing house will enter into a contract with the writer. In some cases, the editor will prepare that contract; in others, the contract will be prepared by the publisher or someone else at the publishing house. The contract will specify when the manuscript is due, how much the author will be paid, how long the manuscript must be, and what will happen if the author cannot deliver a manuscript that the editor believes is suitable for publication, among other things.

After the contract has been signed, the writer will begin work. The acquisitions editor must keep track of the author's progress. Publishing budgets must be prepared in advance so that vendors can be paid and books can be advertised, so it is important that the manuscript be delivered by the due date. Some authors work well on their own and complete their work efficiently and effectively. In many cases, however, authors have problems. They may need advice from the editor regarding content, style, or organization of information. Often, the editor will want to see parts of the manuscript as they are completed. That way, any problems in the writer's work can be identified and solved as soon as possible.

Some typical problems are statements the writer makes that may leave the publisher open to charges of libel or plagiarism. If this problem arises, the editor will require the writer to revise the manuscript. If the writer uses materials that were created by other people (such as long quotations, tables, or artwork), it may be necessary to request permission to use those materials. If permission is required but is not given, the materials cannot be used. It is usually the author's job to obtain permission, but sometimes that task is performed by the editor. In any case, the editor must make sure that necessary permissions are obtained. When an acceptable manuscript has been delivered, the acquisition editor's job is usually complete.

Some publishing houses have editors who specialize in working with authors. These *developmental editors* do not acquire manuscripts. Instead, they make sure the author stays on schedule and does a good job of organizing material and writing.

Once an acceptable manuscript has been delivered to the publishing house, it is turned over to a *copy editor*. This editor's job is to read the manuscript carefully and make sure that it is sufficiently well written, factually correct (sometimes this job is done by a *researcher* or *fact checker*), grammatically correct, and appropriate in tone and style for its intended readers. If a book is not well written, it is not likely to be well received by readers. If it is not factually correct, it will not be taken seriously by those who spot its errors. If it is not grammatically correct, it will not be understood. If it is not appropriate for its audience, it will be utterly useless. Any errors or problems in a printed piece reflect badly not only on the author but also on the publishing house.

The copy editor must be an expert in the English language, have a keen eye for detail, and know how to identify problems. The editor will simply correct some kinds of errors, but in some cases—especially when the piece deals with specialized material—the editor may need to ask, or query, the author about certain points. An editor must never change something that he or she does not understand, since one of the worst errors an editor can make is to change something that is correct to something that is incorrect.

After the manuscript has been edited by the copy editor, it may be (but is not always) sent to the author for review. When the editor and author have agreed on the final copy, the editor or another specialist will use various kinds of coding to mark the manuscript for typesetting. The codes, which usually correlate to information provided by a *graphic designer*, tell the *typesetter* which typefaces to use, how large to make the type, what the layout of the finished pages will look like, and where illustrations or other visual materials will be placed on the pages, among other things.

After the manuscript has been typeset and turned into galley proofs, or typeset copy that has not been divided into pages, the galleys are usually sent to the author to be checked. If the author finds errors or requests that changes be made, the copy editor or the *production editor* will oversee the process, determining which changes will be made.

Managing the editorial staff is the job of the *managing editor*, who draws up budgets for projects, oversees schedules, assigns projects to other editors, and ensures that the editorial staff is working efficiently. The managing editor's boss is the *editor-in-chief*, *editorial director,* or *executive editor*. This editor works closely with the publisher, determining the kinds of materials the house will publish and ensuring that the editorial staff carries out the wishes of the publisher. The editor-in-chief and managing editor also work closely with the heads of other departments, such as marketing, sales, and production.

The basic functions performed by *magazine and newspaper editors* are much like those performed by book editors, but a significant amount of the writing that appears in magazines and newspapers, or periodicals, is done by staff writers. Periodicals often use editors who specialize in specific areas, such as *city editors*, who oversee the work of reporters who specialize in local news, and department editors. *Department editors* specialize in areas such as business, fashion, sports, and features, to name only a few. These departments are determined by the interests of the audience that the periodical intends to reach. Like book houses, periodicals use copy editors, researchers, and fact checkers, but at small periodicals, one or a few editors may be responsible for tasks that would be performed by many people at a larger publication.

Requirements

High School

Editors must be expert communicators, so you should excel in English if you wish to be an editor. You must learn to write extremely well, since you will be correcting and even rewriting the work of others. If elective classes in writing are available in your school, take them. Study journalism and take communications courses. Work as a writer or editor for the school paper. Take a photography class. Since virtually all editors use computers, take computer courses. You absolutely must learn to type. If you cannot type accurately and rapidly, you will be at an extreme disadvantage. Don't forget, however, that a successful editor must have a wide range of knowledge. The more you know about many areas, the more likely you will be to do well as an editor. Don't hesitate to explore areas that you find interesting. Do everything you can to satisfy your intellectual curiosity. As far as most editors are concerned, there is no useless information.

Postsecondary Training

An editor must have a bachelor's degree, and advanced degrees are highly recommended for book editors and magazine editors. Most editors have degrees in English or journalism, but it is not unheard of for editors to major in other liberal arts. If you know that you want to specialize in a field such as scientific editing, you may wish to major in the area of science of your choice while minoring in English, writing, or journalism. There are many opportunities for editors in technical fields, since most of those who go into editing are interested primarily in the liberal arts. Many colleges offer courses in book editing, magazine design, general editing, and writing. Some colleges, such as the University of Chicago and Stanford University, offer programs in publishing, and many magazines and newspapers offer internships to students. Take advantage of these opportunities. It is extremely important that you gain some practical experience while you are in school. Work on the school paper or find a part-time job with a newspaper or magazine. Don't hesitate to work for a publication in a noneditorial position. The more you know about the publishing business, the better off you will be.

Other Requirements

Good editors are fanatics. Their passion for good writing comes close to the point of obsession. They are analytical people who know how to think clearly and communicate what they are thinking. They read widely. They not only recognize good English when they see it but also know what makes it good. If they read something they don't understand, they analyze it until they do understand it. If they see a word they don't know, they look it up. When they are curious about something, they take action and research the subject. They are not satisfied with not knowing things.

You must be detail oriented to succeed as an editor. You must also be patient, since you may have to spend hours turning a few pages of near-gibberish into powerful, elegant English. If you are the kind of person who can't sit still, you probably will not succeed as an editor. To be a good editor, you must be a self-starter who is not afraid to make decisions. You must be good not only at identifying problems but also at solving them, so you must be creative. If you are both creative and a perfectionist, editing may be the line of work for you.

Exploring

One of the best ways to explore the field of editing is to work on a school newspaper or other publication. The experience you gain will definitely be helpful, even if your duties are not strictly editorial. Being involved in writing, reporting, typesetting, proofreading, printing, or any other task related to publishing will help you to understand editing and how it relates to the entire field of publishing.

If you cannot work for the school paper, try to land a part-time job on a local newspaper or newsletter. If that doesn't work, you might want to publish your own newsletter. There is nothing like trying to put together a small publication to make you understand how publishing works. You may try combining another interest with your interest in editing. For example, if you are interested in environmental issues, you might want to start a newsletter that deals with environmental problems and solutions in your community. Use your imagination.

Another useful project is keeping a journal. In fact, any writing project will be helpful, since editing and writing are inextricably linked. Write something every day. Try to rework your writing until it is as good as you can make it. Write about anything that you find interesting. Write letters to the editor, short stories, poetry, essays—anything you like.

Employers

One of the best things about the field of editing is that there are many kinds of opportunities for editors. The most obvious employers for editors are book publishers, magazines, and newspapers. There are many varieties of all three of these types of publishers. There are small and large publishers, general and specialized publishers, local and national publishers. If you have a strong interest in a particular field, you will undoubtedly find various publishers that specialize in it.

Another excellent source of employment is business. Almost all businesses of any size need writers and editors on a full-time or part-time basis. Corporations often publish newsletters for their employees or produce publications that talk about how they do business. Large companies produce annual reports that must be written and edited. In addition, advertising is a major source of work for editors, proofreaders, and writers. Advertising agencies use editors, proofreaders, and quality-control people, as do typesetting and printing companies (in many cases, proofreaders edit as well as proofread). Keep in mind that somebody has to work on all the printed material you see every day, from books and magazines to menus and matchbooks.

Starting Out

There is tremendous competition for editorial jobs, so it is important for a beginner who wishes to break into the business to be as well prepared as possible. College students who have gained experience as interns, have worked for publications during the summers, or have attended special programs in publishing will be at an advantage. In addition, applicants for any editorial position must be extremely careful when preparing cover letters and resumes. Even a single error in spelling or usage will disqualify an applicant.

Applicants for editorial or proofreading positions must also expect to take and pass tests that are designed to determine their language skills.

Many editors enter the field as editorial assistants or proofreaders. Some editorial assistants perform only clerical tasks, whereas others may also proofread or perform basic editorial tasks. Typically, an editorial assistant who performs well will be given the opportunity to take on more and more editorial duties as time passes. Proofreaders have the advantage of being able to look at the work of editors, so they can learn while they do their own work.

Good sources of information about job openings are school placement offices, classified ads in newspapers and trade journals, specialized publications such as *Publishers Weekly* (a good source of jobs in book publishing), and Internet sites. One way to proceed is to identify local publishers through the Yellow Pages. Many publishers have Web sites that list job openings, and large publishers often have telephone job lines that serve the same purpose.

Advancement

In book houses, employees who start as editorial assistants or proofreaders and show promise generally become copy editors. After gaining skill in that position, they may be given a wider range of duties while retaining the same title. The next step may be a position as a senior copy editor, which involves overseeing the work of junior copy editors, or as a *project editor*. The project editor performs a wide variety of tasks, including copyediting, coordinating the work of in-house and freelance copy editors, and managing the schedule of a particular project. From this position, an editor may move up to become first assistant editor, then managing editor, then editor-in-chief. These positions involve more management and decision making than is usually found in the positions described previously. The editor-in-chief works with the publisher to ensure that a suitable editorial policy is being followed, while the managing editor is responsible for all aspects of the editorial department. The assistant editor provides support to the managing editor.

Newspaper editors generally begin working on the copy desk, where they progress from less significant stories and projects to major news and feature stories. A common route to advancement is for copy editors to be promoted to a particular department, where they may move up the ranks to management positions. An editor who has achieved success in a department may become a city editor, who is responsible for news, or a managing editor, who runs the entire editorial operation of a newspaper.

Magazine editors advance in much the same way that book editors do. After they become copy editors, they work their way up to become senior editors, managing editors, and editors-in-chief. In many cases, magazine editors advance by moving from a position on one magazine to the same position with a larger or more prestigious magazine. Such moves often bring significant increases in both pay and status.

Earnings

Although a small percentage of editors are paid extremely well, the average editor is not well paid. Competition for editing jobs is fierce, and there is no shortage of people who wish to enter the field. For that reason, companies that employ editors generally pay relatively low wages.

In July of 1998, *Publishers Weekly*, an important source of information about the book business, published a salary survey that stated that entry-level positions generally pay between $25,000 and $45,000, more advanced positions pay between $52,000 and $53,800, and supervisory positions pay between $45,000 and $88,700. It is worth noting that the vast majority of beginning editors will be paid salaries that are in line with the lower end of the range quoted above. Beginning salaries in the teens and low twenties are still common in many areas. The salaries of magazine editors are roughly comparable to those of book editors.

According to the Dow Jones Newspaper Fund, the average beginning salary for an editorial assistant was $21,000 in 1996, and it is reasonable to assume that that figure has not increased significantly. The Newspaper Guild has estimated that editors with at least five years of experience averaged more than $30,000 in 1996, while senior editors at large papers made more than $67,000 per year. Salaries for book and magazine editors were similar to those of newspaper editors.

According to the *Occupational Outlook Handbook*, median annual earnings for writers and editors, including technical writers, were $36,480 in 1998. The lowest 10 percent earned less than $20,920 and the highest 10 percent earned over $76,600.

Technical editors usually make more money than newspaper, magazine, or book editors. In 1996, the median salary for technical writers was $44,000, according to the Technical Communicators Salary Survey, and it is likely that the figure for technical editors was similar. The U.S. Department of Labor's *Occupational Outlook Handbook* has estimated that the average salary earned in 1997 by technical writers and editors in computer data and processing services was $39,200.

Work Environment

The environments in which editors work vary widely. For the most part, publishers of all kinds realize that a quiet atmosphere is conducive to work that requires tremendous concentration. It takes an unusual ability to focus to edit in a noisy place. Most editors work in private offices or cubicles. Book editors often work in quieter surroundings than do newspaper editors or quality-control people in advertising agencies, who sometimes work in rather loud and hectic situations.

Even in relatively quiet surroundings, however, editors often have many distractions. A project editor who is trying to do some copyediting or review the editing of others may, for example, have to deal with phone calls from authors, questions from junior editors, meetings with members of the editorial and production staff, and questions from freelancers, among many other distractions. In many cases, editors have computers that are exclusively for their own use, but in others, editors must share computers that are located in a common area.

Deadlines are an important issue for virtually all editors. Newspaper and magazine editors work in a much more pressurized atmosphere than book editors because they face daily or weekly deadlines, whereas book production usually takes place over several months.

In almost all cases, editors must work long hours during certain phases of the editing process. Some newspaper editors start work at 5 AM, others work until 11 PM or even through the night. Feature editors, columnists, and editorial page editors usually can schedule their day in a more regular fashion, as can editors who work on weekly newspapers. Editors working on hard news, however, may receive an assignment that must be completed, even if work extends well into the next shift.

Outlook

According to the *Occupational Outlook Handbook*, employment of editors will increase faster than the average through 2008. At the same time, however, competition for those jobs will remain intense, since so many people want to enter the field. Book publishing will remain particularly competitive, since many people still view the field in a romantic light. Much of the expansion in publishing is expected to occur in small newspapers, radio stations, and television stations. In these organizations, pay is low even by the standards of the publishing business.

One of the major trends in publishing is specialization. More and more publishing ventures are targeting relatively narrow markets, which means that there are more opportunities for editors to combine their work and their personal interests. It is also true, however, that many of these specialty publications do not survive for long.

There will be increasing job opportunities for editors in Internet publishing as online publishing and services continue to grow. Advertising and public relations will also provide employment opportunities.

A fairly large number of positions—both full time and freelance—become available when experienced editors leave the business for other fields. Many editors make this decision because they find that they can make more money in other businesses than they can as editors.

For More Information

The following organization is an excellent source of information about careers in copyediting. The ACES organizes educational seminars and maintains lists of internships.

American Copy Editors Society (ACES)
3 Healy Street
Huntington, NY 11743
Tel: 800-393-7681
Web: http://www.copydesk.org

The AAP is an organization of book publishers. Its extensive Web site is a good place to begin learning about the book business.

Association of American Publishers (AAP)
71 Fifth Avenue
New York, NY 10010-2368
Tel: 212-255-0200
Email: aphillips@publishers.org
Web: http://www.publishers.org

This organization provides information about internships and the newspaper business in general.

Dow Jones Newspaper Fund
PO Box 300
Princeton, NJ 08543-0300
Tel: 609-452-2820
Email: newsfund@wsj.dowjones.com
Web: http://www.dowjones.com/newsfund/

The EFA is an organization for freelance editors. Members receive a newsletter and a free listing in their directory.

Editorial Freelancers Association (EFA)
71 West 23rd Street, Suite 1504
New York, NY 10010
Tel: 212-929-5400
Web: http://www.the-efa.org

The MPA is a good source of information about internships.

Magazine Publishers of America (MPA)
919 Third Avenue, 22nd Floor
New York, NY 10022
Tel: 212-872-3700
Web: http://www.magazine.org

The Slot is a Web site founded and maintained by Bill Walsh, financial copy desk chief at The Washington Post. One of its most significant features is The Curmudgeon's Stylebook, a user-friendly guide to style and usage.

The Slot
Web: http://www.theslot.com

Foreign Correspondents

	School Subjects
English Foreign language	

	Personal Skills
Communication/ideas Helping/teaching	

	Work Environment
Indoors and outdoors Primarily multiple locations	

	Minimum Education Level
Bachelor's degree	

	Salary Range
$50,000 to $75,000 to $100,000	

	Certification or Licensing
None available	

	Outlook
Little change or more slowly than the average	

Overview

Foreign correspondents report on news from countries outside of where their newspapers, radio or television networks, or wire services are located. Foreign correspondents sometimes work for a particular newspaper, but since today's media are more interested in local and national news, they usually rely on reports from news wire services to handle international news coverage rather than dispatching their own reporters to the scene. Only the biggest newspapers and television networks employ foreign correspondents. These reporters are usually stationed in a particular city and cover a wide territory.

History

James Gordon Bennett, Sr. (1795-1872), a prominent United States journalist and publisher of the *New York Herald*, was responsible for many firsts in the newspaper industry. He was the first publisher to sell papers through newsboys, the first to use illustrations for news stories, the first to publish stock-market prices and daily financial articles, and he was the first to employ European correspondents. Bennett's son, James Gordon Bennett, Jr. (1841-1918), carried on the family business and in 1871 sent Henry M. Stanley to central Africa to find Dr. David Livingstone.

In the early days, even magazines employed foreign correspondents. Famous American poet Ezra Pound, for example, reported from London for *Poetry* and *The Little Review*.

The inventions of the telegraph, telephone, typewriter, portable type-writer, and the portable laptop computer all have contributed to the field of foreign correspondence.

The Job

The foreign correspondent is stationed in a foreign country where his or her job is to report on the news there. Foreign news can range from the violent (wars, coups, and refugee situations) to the calm (cultural events and financial issues). Although a domestic correspondent is responsible for covering specific areas of the news like politics, health, sports, consumer affairs, business, or religion, foreign correspondents are responsible for all of these areas in the country where they are stationed. A China-based correspondent, for example, could spend a day covering the new trade policy between the United States and China, and the next day report on the religious persecution of Christians by the Chinese government.

A foreign correspondent often is responsible for more than one country. Depending on where he or she is stationed, the foreign correspondent might have to act as a one-person band in gathering and preparing stories.

"There are times when the phone rings at five in the morning and you're told to go to Pakistan," said Michael Lev, Tokyo Bureau Chief for the *Chicago Tribune*. "You must keep your wits about you and figure out what to do next."

For the most part, Lev decides on his own story ideas, choosing which ones interest him the most out of a myriad of possibilities. But foreign correspondents alone are responsible for getting the story done, and unlike reporters back home, they have little or no support staff to help them. Broadcast foreign correspondents, for example, after filming scenes may have to do their own audio editing. And just like other news reporters, foreign correspondents work under the pressure of deadlines. In addition, they often are thrown into unfamiliar situations in strange places.

Part of the importance of a foreign correspondent's job is keeping readers or viewers aware of the various cultures and practices held by the rest of the world. Lev says he tries to focus on similarities and differences between the Asian countries he covers and the United States. "If you don't understand another culture, you are more likely to come into conflict with it," he says.

Foreign correspondents are drawn to conflicts of all kinds, especially war. They may choose to go to the front of a battle to get an accurate picture of what's happening. Or they may be able to get the story from a safer position. Sometimes they face weapons trained directly on them.

Much of a foreign correspondent's time is spent doing research, investigating leads, setting up appointments, making travel arrangements, making on-site observations, and interviewing local people or those involved in the situation. The foreign correspondent often must be experienced in taking photographs or shooting video.

Living conditions can be rough or primitive, sometimes with no running water. The job can prove isolating.

After correspondents have interviewed sources and noted observations about an event or filmed it, they put their stories together, writing on computers and using modern technology like the Internet, email, satellite telephones, and fax machines to finish the job and transmit the story to their newspaper, broadcast station, or wire service. Many times, correspondents work out of hotel rooms.

Requirements

High School

In addition to English and creative writing needed for a career in journalism, you should study languages, social studies, political science, history, and geography. Initial experience may be gained by working on your school newspaper or yearbook, or taking advantage of study-abroad programs.

Postsecondary Training

In college, obtaining a journalism major is helpful but may not be crucial to obtaining a job as a foreign correspondent. Classes, or even a major, in political science or literature could be beneficial. Economics and foreign languages also help.

Other Requirements

To be a foreign correspondent, in addition to a definite love of adventure, you need curiosity about how other people live, diplomacy when interviewing people, courage to sometimes confront people on uncomfortable topics, ability to communicate well, and the discipline to sometimes act as your own boss. You also need to be strong enough to hold up under pressure yet flexible enough to adapt to other cultures.

Employers

Foreign correspondents work for news wire services, such as the Associated Press, Reuters, and Agence-France Press, major metropolitan newspapers, news magazines, and television and radio networks. These media are located in the nation's largest cities and in the case of Reuters and Agence-France Press, in Europe.

Starting Out

College graduates have a couple of paths to choose between to become a foreign correspondent. They can decide to experience what being a foreign correspondent is like immediately by going to a country, perhaps one whose language is familiar to them, and freelancing or working as a stringer. That means writing stories and offering them to anyone who will buy them. This method can be hard to accomplish financially in the short run but can pay off substantially in the long run.

This is the route Judith Matloff, foreign correspondent for *The Christian Science Monitor,* took. She started out freelancing in Mexico for English-speaking newspapers, publications, and wire services. Nine months after selling her first freelance article, the wire service Reuters offered her a job and her career took off.

Another path is to take the traditional route of a journalist and try to get hired upon graduation at any newspaper, radio station, or television station you can. It helps in this regard to have worked at a summer internship during your college years. Recent college graduates generally get hired at small newspapers or media stations, although a few major metropolitan dailies will employ top graduates for a year with no guarantee of them being kept on afterward. After building experience at a small paper or station, a reporter can try to find work at progressively bigger ones. Reporters who find employment at a major metropolitan daily that uses foreign correspondents can work their way through the ranks to become one. This is the path Lev took and he became a foreign correspondent when he was in his early 30s. He suggests that working for a wire service may allow a reporter to get abroad faster, but he thinks more freedom can be found working for a newspaper.

Advancement

Foreign correspondents can advance to other locations that are more appealing to them or that offer a bigger challenge. Or they can return home to become columnists, editorial writers, editors, or network news directors.

Earnings

Salaries vary greatly depending on the publication, network, or station, and the cost of living and tax structure in various places around the world where foreign correspondents work. Generally, salaries range from $50,000 to an average of about $75,000 to a peak of $100,000 or more. Some media will pay for living expenses, such as the costs of a home, school for the reporter's children, and a car.

Outlook

Although employment at newspapers, radio stations, and television stations in general is expected to continue to decline, the number of foreign correspondent jobs has leveled off. The employment outlook is expected to remain relatively stable, or even increase should a major conflict or war occur.

Factors that keep the number of foreign correspondents low are the high cost of maintaining a foreign news bureau and the relative lack of interest Americans show in world news. Despite these factors, the number of correspondents is not expected to decrease. There are simply too few as it is;

decreasing the number could put the job in danger of disappearing, which most journalists believe is not an option. For now and the near future, you can expect most job openings to arise from the need to replace those correspondents who leave the job.

For More Information

The ASJA provides information on careers in newspaper reporting, as well as information on education and financial aid.

American Society of Journalists and Authors (ASJA)
1501 Broadway, Suite 302
New York, NY 10036
Tel: 212-997-0947
Email: execdir@asja.org
Web: http://www.asja.org/

The AEJMC provides general educational information on all areas of journalism (newspapers, magazines, television, and radio).

**Association for Education in Journalism
and Mass Communication (AEJMC)**
121 LaConte College
University of South Carolina
Columbia, SC 29208-0251
Tel: 803-777-2006
Email: aejmc@sc.edu
Web: http://www.aejmc.sc.edu/on-line/home.html

The NAB has information on jobs, scholarships, internships, college programs, and other resources. It offers Careers in Radio *($4) and* Careers in Television *($4), which describe the key jobs, educational requirements, and job-related experience required.*

National Association of Broadcasters (NAB)
1771 N Street, NW
Washington, DC 20036
Tel: 202-429-5300
Email: jearnhar@nab.org
Web: http://www.nab.org

The SPJ has student chapters all over the United States. Among its many services to students, it offers information on scholarships and internships.

Society of Professional Journalists (SPJ)
16 South Jackson
Greencastle, IN 46135-0077
Email: spj@link2000.net
Web: http://www.spj.org

Graphic Designers

Art Computer science	School Subjects
Artistic Communication/ideas	Personal Skills
Primarily indoors Primarily one location	Work Environment
Some postsecondary training	Minimum Education Level
$23,000 to $50,000 to $85,000+	Salary Range
None available	Certification or Licensing
Faster than the average	Outlook

Overview

Graphic designers are practical artists whose creations are intended to express ideas, convey information, or draw attention to a product. They design a wide variety of materials including advertisements, displays, packaging, signs, computer graphics and games, book and magazine covers and interiors, animated characters, and company logos to fit the needs and preferences of their various clients.

History

The challenge of combining beauty, function, and technology in whatever form has preoccupied artisans in all periods of history. Graphic design work has been used to create products and promote commerce for as long as people have used symbols, pictures, and typography to communicate ideas.

Graphic design work grew alongside the growth of print media—newspapers, magazines, catalogs, and advertising. Typically, the graphic designer would sketch several rough drafts of the layout of pictures and words. After one of the drafts was approved, the designer would complete a final layout including detailed type and artwork specifications. The words were sent to a typesetter and the artwork assigned to an illustrator. When the final pieces were returned, the designer or a keyline and paste-up artist would adhere them with rubber cement or wax to an illustration board. Different colored items were placed on acetate overlays. This camera-ready art was now ready to be sent to a printer for photographing and reproduction.

Computer technology has revolutionized the way many graphic designers do their work: today it is possible to be a successful graphic designer even if you can't draw more than simple stick figures. Graphic designers are now able to draw, color, and revise the many different images they work with daily. They can choose typefaces, size type, and place it without having to align it on the page using a T-square and triangle. Computer graphics enable graphic designers to work more quickly, since details like size, shape, and color are easy to change.

Graphics programs for computers are continually revised and improved, moving more and more design work from the artist's table to the computer mousepad and graphics tablet. This area of computer technology is booming now and will be in the future, as computer graphics and multimedia move toward virtual reality applications. Many graphic designers with solid computer experience will be needed to work with these systems.

The Job

Graphic designers are not primarily fine artists, although they may be highly skilled at drawing or painting. Most designs commissioned to graphic designers involve both artwork and copy (that is, words). Thus, the designer must not only be familiar with the wide range of art media (photography, drawing, painting, collage, etc.) and styles, but he or she must also be familiar with a wide range of typefaces and know how to manipulate them for the right effect. Because design tends to change in a similar way to fashion, designers must keep up to date with the latest trends. At the same time, they must be well grounded in more traditional, classic designs.

Graphic designers can work as in-house designers for a particular company, as staff designers for a graphic design firm, or as freelance designers working for themselves. Some designers specialize in designing advertising materials or packaging. Others focus on corporate identity materials such as company stationery and logos. Some work mainly for publishers designing book and magazine covers and page layouts. Some work in the area of computer graphics, creating still or animated graphics for computer software, videos, or motion pictures. A highly specialized type of graphic designer, the environmental graphic designer, designs large outdoor signs. Some graphic designers design exclusively on the computer, while others may use both the computer and traditional hand drawings or paintings, depending on the project's needs and requirements.

Whatever the specialty and whatever their medium, all graphic designers take a similar approach to a project, whether it is for an entirely new design or for a variation on an existing one. Graphic designers begin by determining as best they can the needs and preferences of the clients and the potential users, buyers, or viewers.

In the case of a graphic designer working on a company logo, for example, he or she will likely meet with company representatives to discuss such points as how and where the company is going to use the logo and what size, color, and shape preferences company executives might have. Project budgets must be carefully respected: a design that may be perfect in every way but that is too costly to reproduce is basically useless. Graphic designers may need to compare their ideas with similar ones from other companies and analyze the image they project. Thus they must have a good knowledge of how various colors, shapes, and layouts affect the viewer psychologically.

After a plan has been conceived and the details worked out, the graphic designer does some preliminary designs (generally two or three) to present to the client for approval. The client may reject the preliminary design entirely and request a new design, or he or she may ask the designer to make alterations to the existing design. The designer then goes back to the drawing board to attempt a new design or make the requested changes. This process continues until the client approves the design.

Once a design has been approved, the graphic designer prepares the design for professional reproduction, that is, printing. The printer may require a "mechanical," in which the artwork and copy are arranged on a white board just as it is to be photographed, or the designer may be asked to submit an electronic copy of the design. Either way, designers must have a good understanding of the printing process, including color separation, paper properties, and halftone (i.e., photograph) reproduction.

Requirements

High School

High school students should take any art and design courses that are available. Computer classes are also helpful, particularly those that teach page layout programs or art and photography manipulation programs. Working on the school newspaper or yearbook can provide valuable design experience. You may also volunteer to design flyers or posters for school events.

Postsecondary Training

More graphic designers are recognizing the value of formal training, and at least two out of three people entering the field today have a college degree or some college education. Over one hundred colleges and art schools offer graphic design programs that are accredited by the National Association of Schools of Art and Design. At many schools, graphic design students must take a year of basic art and design courses before being accepted into the bachelor's degree program. In addition, applicants to the bachelor's degree programs in graphic arts may be asked to submit samples of their work to prove artistic ability. Many schools and employers depend on samples, or portfolios, to evaluate the applicants' skills in graphic design.

Many programs increasingly emphasize the importance of using computers for design work. Computer proficiency among graphic designers will be very important in the years to come. Interested individuals should select an academic program that incorporates computer training into the curriculum, or train themselves on their own.

A bachelor of fine arts program at a four-year college or university may include courses such as principles of design, art and art history, painting, sculpture, mechanical and architectural drawing, architecture, computerized design, basic engineering, fashion designing and sketching, garment construction, and textiles. Such degrees are desirable but not always necessary for obtaining a position as a graphic designer.

Other Requirements

As with all artists, graphic designers need a degree of artistic talent, creativity, and imagination. They must be sensitive to beauty and have an eye for detail and a strong sense of color, balance, and proportion. To a great extent, these qualities are natural, but they can be developed through training, both on the job and in professional schools, colleges, and universities.

More and more graphic designers need solid computer skills and working knowledge of several of the common drawing, image editing, and page layout programs. Graphic design on the computer is done on both Macintosh systems and on PC systems; many designers have both types of computers in their studios.

With or without specialized education, graphic designers seeking employment should have a good portfolio containing samples of their best work. The graphic designer's portfolio is extremely important and can make a difference when an employer must choose between two otherwise equally qualified candidates.

A period of on-the-job training is expected for all beginning designers. The length of time it takes to become fully qualified as a graphic designer may run from one to three years, depending on prior education and experience as well as innate talent.

Exploring

High school students interested in a career in graphic design have a number of ways to find out whether they have the talent, ambition, and perseverance to succeed in the field. Students should take as many art and design courses as possible while still in high school and should become proficient at working on computers. In addition, to get an insider's view of various design occupations, they could enlist the help of art teachers or school guidance counselors to make arrangements to tour design companies and interview designers.

While studying, students interested in graphic design can get practical experience by participating in school and community projects that call for design talents. These might include such activities as building sets for plays, setting up exhibits, planning seasonal and holiday displays, and preparing programs and other printed materials. For those interested in publication design, work on the school newspaper or yearbook is invaluable.

Part-time and summer jobs offer would-be designers an excellent way to become familiar with the day-to-day requirements of a particular design occupation and gain some basic related experience. Possible places of employment include design studios, design departments in advertising agencies and manufacturing companies, department and furniture stores, flower shops, workshops that produce ornamental items, and museums. Museums also use a number of volunteer workers. Inexperienced people are often employed as sales, clerical, or general helpers; those with a little more education and experience may qualify for jobs in which they have a chance to develop actual design skills and build portfolios of completed design projects.

Employers

Graphic designers work in many different industries, including the wholesale and retail trade (department stores, furniture and home furnishings stores, apparel stores, florist shops); manufacturing industries (machinery, motor vehicles and aircraft, metal products, instruments, apparel, textiles, printing and publishing); service industries (business services, engineering, architecture); construction firms; and government agencies. Public relations and publicity firms, advertising agencies, commercial printers, and mail-order houses all have graphic design departments. The publishing industry is a primary employer of graphic designers, including book publishers, magazines, newspapers, and newsletters. Many graphic designers are self-employed, and hire their freelance services to multiple clients.

Starting Out

The best way to enter the field of graphic design is to have a strong portfolio. Potential employers rely on portfolios to evaluate talent and how that talent might be used to fit the company's special needs. Beginning graphic designers can assemble a portfolio from work completed at school, in art classes, and in part-time or freelance jobs. The portfolio should continually be updated to reflect the designer's growing skills, so it will always be ready for possible job changes.

Job interviews may be obtained by applying directly to companies that employ designers. Many colleges and professional schools have placement services to help their graduates find positions, and sometimes it is possible to get a referral from a previous part-time employer or volunteer coordinator.

Advancement

As part of their on-the-job training, beginning graphic designers generally are given the simpler tasks and work under direct supervision. As they gain experience, they move up to more complex work with increasingly less supervision.

Experienced graphic designers, especially those with leadership capabilities, may be promoted to chief designer, design department head, or other supervisory positions.

Computer graphic designers can move into other computer-related positions with additional education. Some may become interested in graphics programming in order to further improve computer design capabilities. Others may want to become involved with multimedia and interactive graphics. Video games, touch-screen displays in stores, and even laser light shows are all products of multimedia graphic designers.

When designers develop personal styles that are in high demand in the marketplace, they sometimes go into business for themselves. Freelance design work can be erratic, however, so usually only the most experienced designers with an established client base can count on consistent full-time work.

Earnings

The range of salaries for graphic designers is quite broad. Many earn as little as $17,000, while others receive more than $35,000. Salaries depend primarily on the nature and scope of the employer, with computer graphic designers earning wages on the high end of the range.

Self-employed designers can earn a lot one year and substantially more or less the next. Their earnings depend on individual talent and business ability, but, in general, are higher than those of salaried designers, although like any self-employed individual, they must pay their own insurance costs and taxes and are not compensated for vacation or sick days.

The Society of Publication Designers has estimated that entry-level graphic designers earned between $23,000 and $27,000 annually in 1997. Salaried designers who advance to the position of design manager or design director earn about $60,000 a year and, at the level of corporate vice-president, make $70,000 and up. The owner of a consulting firm can make $85,000 or more.

Graphic designers who work for large corporations receive full benefits, including health insurance, paid vacation, and sick leave.

Work Environment

Most graphic designers work regular hours in clean, comfortable, pleasant offices or studios. Conditions vary depending on the design specialty.

Some graphic designers work in small establishments with few employees; others, in large organizations with large design departments. Some deal mostly with their co-workers; others may have a lot of public contact. Freelance designers are paid by the assignment. To maintain a steady income, they must constantly strive to please their clients and to find new ones.

Computer graphic designers may have to work long, irregular hours in order to complete an especially ambitious project.

Outlook

Chances for employment look very good for qualified graphic designers through 2008, especially for those involved with computer graphics. The design field in general is expected to grow at a faster than average rate. As computer graphic technology continues to advance, there will be a need for well-trained computer graphic designers. Companies that have always used graphics will expect their designers to perform work on computers. Companies for which graphic design was once too time consuming or costly are now sprucing up company newsletters and magazines, among other things, and need graphic designers to do it.

Because the design field is a popular one, appealing to many talented individuals, competition is expected to be strong in all areas. Beginners and designers with only average talent or without formal education and technical skills may encounter some difficulty in securing employment.

About one-third of all graphic designers are self-employed, a higher proportion than is found in most other occupations.

For More Information

For more information about careers in graphic design, contact:

American Center for Design
233 East Ontario, Suite 500
Chicago, IL 60611
Tel: 312-787-2018

American Institute of Graphic Arts
164 Fifth Avenue
New York, NY 10160-1652
Tel: 800-548-1634
Email. aiganatl@aol.com
Web: http://www.aiga.org

National Association of Schools of Art and Design
11250 Roger Bacon Drive, Suite 21
Reston, VA 22090
Tel: 703-437-0700

Society for Environmental Graphic Design
1 Story Street
Cambridge, MA 02138
Tel: 617-868-3381

Society of Publication Designers
60 East 42nd Street, Suite 721
New York, NY 10165
Tel: 212-983-8585
Web: http://www.spd.org/

Urban Art International
PO Box 868
Tiburon, CA 94920
Tel: 415-435-5767
Web: http://www.imagesite.com

Indexers

	School Subjects
Computer science	
English	

	Personal Skills
Communication/ideas	
Helping/teaching	

	Work Environment
Primarily indoors	
Primarily one location	

	Minimum Education Level
Bachelor's degree	

	Salary Range
$20,000 to $30,000 to $70,000	

	Certification or Licensing
None available	

	Outlook
About as fast as the average	

Overview

Indexers compile organized lists, called indexes, that help people locate information in a text or body of work. Indexes are like "road maps" that help users find desired information. Just as a map allows travelers to select the most direct route to a destination, indexes should provide users with a basis for selecting relevant information and screening out that which is unwanted.

History

The first known finding list was compiled by Callimachus, a Greek poet and scholar of the 3rd century BC, to provide a guide to the contents of the Alexandrian Library. Primitive alphabetical indexes began to appear in the 16th century AD. In 1614, the bishop of Petina, Antonio Zara, included an index in his *Anatomia ingeniorum etscientiarum* (Anatomy of Talents and Sciences), and in 1677, Johann Jacob Hoffman added an index to his *Lexicon universale*. These early indexes were difficult to use because entries under each letter of the alphabet were not arranged alphabetically. Every term beginning with a "B" would appear somewhere under that letter, but subjects beginning "Ba" did not necessarily precede those beginning "Be."

In the 18th century, alphabetic indexing improved, as demonstrated in Denis Diderot's (1713-84) *Encyclopedie*, which is alphabetized consistently throughout. In the 19th century, indexers attempted to compile indexes that covered entire fields of knowledge. The *Reader's Guide to Periodic Literature*, published by H.W. Wilson Company of New York, is one of the best-known examples of an index that includes references to many publications.

The 20th century revolutionized the fields of indexing and information retrieval by introducing computer technology. There are now many computer programs designed to assist in the preparation of indexes. Some programs, in fact, have largely automated the mechanical aspects of indexing.

The Job

There are several types of common indexes. The most familiar is the back-of-book index. *Back-of-book indexes* contain references to information in only one volume. Most nonfiction, single-volume texts include this sort of index. Multivolume indexes contain references to information in more than one volume. The page references in a multivolume index must indicate clearly both the volume number and the page number of the cited information. Most encyclopedias include multivolume indexes. Magazines and newspapers also have indexes. These *periodical indexes* are published separately, at regular intervals throughout the year, and are extremely helpful to researchers.

A more recent development in indexing is the *online index*. Online indexes help users locate specific information from within a large database. Online indexes differ from a simple search function in that an indexer has created a translational thesaurus. When a user inputs a term that actually does not exist in the database, the online index will translate the term to a synonym that does exist so that the user may access the needed information.

Though their scope and purposes vary widely, all indexes have certain features in common. Every index must be organized according to a useful system. Most indexes are alphabetical, though in some specialized cases they may be chronological or numerical. The index to a history text, for instance, might be in chronological order. The two most commonly used alphabetical filing systems are the word-by-word arrangement, under which New York would precede Newark, and the letter-by-letter arrangement, under which New York would follow Newark.

All indexes must contain index terms, called headings, and page numbers or other locators. Most indexes also contain subheadings that help users narrow their search for information. Under the main heading "George Washington," for example, an indexer might use subheadings to separate references to the Revolutionary War from those to Washington's presidency. An index also may include cross-references to other pertinent headings or indicate the presence of illustrations, charts, and bibliographies.

Whether one creates an index on three-by-five index cards or with the help of a software program, the mental process is the same. The indexer first must read and understand the primary information in the text. Only then can the indexer begin to identify key terms and concepts. The second phase in compiling an index is called *tracing*—marking terms or concepts. Choosing appropriate headings is often the most challenging aspect of an indexer's job. Subjects must be indexed not only under the terms used in the text, but also under the terms that may occur to the reader. Since the indexer's first obligation is to help the reader find information, the best indexers ask themselves, "Where would the reader look?"

After tracing, the indexer begins to compile the headings and page references. Entries with many page citations must be divided further by subheadings. The final step in creating an index is editing. The indexer must view the index as a whole in order to polish the organization, delete trivial references, and add appropriate subheadings.

While indexers may organize information by key words or concepts, the most useful indexes usually combine both systems. Key word compilation is indiscriminate and is of limited usefulness to the reader. Key word lists include every instance of a term and usually fail to make connections between synonymous or related terms. Computer programs that promise automated indexing are actually capable only of compiling such key word concordances. In conceptual indexing, on the other hand, the indexer is not bound to standardized terminology, but recognizes synonymous or related information and disregards trivial references. Even the most sophisticated computer program is incapable of creating an adequate conceptual index.

Requirements

High School

Although there is no one educational path that best prepares students to become indexers, a high school diploma and a college degree are necessary. Classes in English and computers are essential, and classes in history and other social sciences will provide familiarity with a broad range of subjects that might be indexed.

Postsecondary Training

Since indexers must be well-read and knowledgeable about a wide range of academic disciplines, a liberal arts degree is highly recommended. Many indexers have one or more advanced degrees as well. Professional training is not required but can be extremely helpful. Though few educational institutions offer indexing courses, many offer relevant classes that may be useful to indexers, such as Information Storage and Retrieval, Introduction to Information Science, and Cataloging and Classification.

Today's indexers must be computer literate to be competitive. Manual preparation of indexes is a dying art due to the widespread availability of computer programs designed to automate the mechanics of indexing. This trend toward computer-assisted indexing will continue as more and more information is created and stored in electronic format. Tomorrow's indexers will often create online indexes for large databases rather than the familiar back-of-book variety. With the incredible proliferation of information in the late 20th century, information management has become an increasingly complex and competitive field. Those who would be indexers must be prepared to adapt rapidly as methods of storing and disseminating information continue to change and advance in the 21st century. With this in mind, aspiring indexers would do well to pursue degrees in library or information science.

Other Requirements

Indexing can be an extremely solitary profession. Indexers should enjoy intellectual challenges and have a passion for coherent structure. To be successful, indexers must also have great patience for detail.

Exploring

To explore the indexing profession, interested high school students should visit libraries to read and evaluate indexes of all kinds. Students also should read some basic books on the practice and theory of indexing, such as *Indexing Books: An Introduction* by Nancy Mulvany or *Indexing from A to Z* by Hans Wellisch. The American Society of Indexers publishes several helpful pamphlets on getting started in the indexing profession. Correspondence courses are available through the U.S. Department of Agriculture.

Employers

Traditionally, indexers have worked for publishers of books or periodicals. Publishers of encyclopedias, legal books, and newspapers usually employ a staff of indexers. They are full-time employees, or they earn a living by freelance indexing. Freelance indexers are self-employed workers who sell their indexing services. Publishers hire freelance indexers to work on specific books or projects.

Starting Out

Novice indexers can enter the field by becoming a junior member of an indexing team at a large publishing house. Beginners commonly work under the close supervision of a more experienced staff member. Freelance indexers begin by soliciting work—a time-consuming and difficult process. In order to gain experience and build client relationships, novice indexers must initially accept small jobs at relatively low pay rates.

Advancement

Junior indexers may advance to positions of greater seniority in two to three years. Eventually, an indexer can attain a supervisory position within an indexing department. Experienced freelance indexers may charge reasonably higher rates as their level of expertise increases.

Earnings

The average salary for a beginning indexer was $20,000 in 1996. More experienced indexers can earn $25,000 to $30,000 as they acquire more supervisory responsibilities and seniority. Freelance indexing has the potential to be more lucrative than in-house indexing, but offers less financial security. Freelance indexers must provide their own offices, equipment, and health insurance. In general, hourly rates more accurately reflect the indexer's efforts than per entry or per page rates because indexes which involve extensive conceptual work may have relatively few entries. Freelance indexers can earn from $20,000 to $70,000 annually, depending on their level of experience.

Work Environment

Full-time indexers usually work between 35 and 40 hours a week in typical office settings. Freelance indexers may work out of their homes or take temporary assignments in the offices of employers. The amount of pressure an indexer experiences varies greatly with the type of indexing. Those who compile indexes for newspapers must sift rapidly through great quantities of information and regularly work long hours. Encyclopedia indexers, on the other hand, may face deadlines only once a year. Freelance indexers have irregular schedules; a freelance indexer may work extremely long hours when completing several projects at once but have relatively little work the following week. In general, freelance indexing is more stressful than in-house work as freelancers must constantly plan out their own work schedules, send invoices, and keep business records, in addition to indexing.

Outlook

Publishers in the 21st century will tend toward computer-assisted indexing, making it necessary for indexers to be well versed in the use of computer programs. Computers are not likely to replace human indexers who have thought-processing abilities anytime soon, however; publishers of reference material, newspapers, and scholarly works will continue to value competent indexers. In addition, as information replaces manufacturing as the world's most valuable industry, new opportunities for indexers should become available.

For More Information

American Society of Indexers
11250 Roger Bacon Drive, Suite 8
Reston, VA 20190-5202
Tel: 703-234-4147
Email: info@asindexing.org
Web: http://www.asindexing.org

Correspondence Study Program
Graduate School, USDA
A.G. Box 9911, Room 1112-South
Washington, DC 20250

Literary Agents

	School Subjects
Business	
English	

	Personal Skills
Communication/ideas	
Leadership/management	

	Work Environment
Primarily indoors	
One location with some travel	

	Minimum Education Level
High school diploma	

	Salary Range
$20,000 to $25,000 to $60,000+	

	Certification or Licensing
None available	

	Outlook
Little change or more slowly than the average	

Overview

Literary agents serve as intermediaries between writers and potential employers such as publishers and television producers. They also represent actors, artists, athletes, musicians, politicians, and other public figures who may seek to undertake writing endeavors. In essence, agents sell a product—their clients' creative talent. In addition to finding work for their clients, agents also may negotiate contracts, pursue publicity, and advise clients in their careers. There are approximately 1,000 independent agents working in the United States, according to the *Occupational Outlook Quarterly*. The majority work in New York, and many others work in Los Angeles, San Francisco, Chicago, and Miami.

History

The business of promoting writers is a product of the 20th century. Modern mass publishing and distribution systems, as well as the advent of the radio, television, and motion picture industries, have created a market for the writer's art that did not exist before. In the past, movie studios used staff writers. Today, independent writers create novels, magazine articles, screenplays, and scripts for readers and videophiles. It was perhaps only appropriate that brokers should emerge to bring together people who need each other: creators and producers. These brokers are literary agents.

The Job

Most agents can be divided into two broad groups: those who represent clients on a case-by-case basis and those who have intensive, ongoing partnerships with clients. Literary agents typically do not have long-term relationships with clients except for established authors. They may work with writers just one time, electing to represent them only after reading manuscripts and determining their viability. Literary agents market their clients' manuscripts to editors, publishers, and television and movie producers, among other buyers. Many of the most prestigious magazines and newspapers will not consider material unless an agent submits it. Busy editors rely on agents to screen manuscripts so that only the best, most professional product reaches them. Sometimes editors go directly to agents with editorial assignments, knowing that the agents will be able to find the best writer for the job.

After taking on a project, such as a book proposal, play, magazine article, or screenplay, agents approach publishers and producers in writing, by phone, or in person and try to convince these decision-makers to use their clients' work. When a publisher or other producer accepts a proposal, agents may negotiate contracts and rights, such as translation and excerpt rights, on behalf of their clients. Rather than pay authors directly, publishers pay their agents, who deduct their commission (anywhere from 4 to 20 percent of the total amount) and return the rest to the author.

Agents who represent established writers perform additional duties for their clients, such as directing them to useful resources, evaluating drafts and offering guidance, speaking for them in matters that must be decided in their absence, and in some instances serving as arbiters between coauthors. Also, to ensure that writers devote as much time as possible to their creative work, agents take care of such business as bookkeeping, processing income checks, and preparing tax forms.

Requirements

High School

High school students who are interested in becoming agents should take classes in literature and composition. Theater and music classes are also beneficial.

Postsecondary Training

Desirable areas of study in college include liberal arts, performing arts, and business administration. It is also helpful to study law, although agents need not be lawyers. A college degree is not necessary, but would-be agents with a college degree are more likely to be hired than those without.

Other Requirements

Agents need not have any specific education or technical skills, but you must have a knack for recognizing and promoting marketable talent. You must be familiar with the needs of publishers so as to approach them with the most appropriate and timely manuscript. You must be persistent without crossing over the line to harassment, for you must not alienate any of the publishers you will want to contact in the future.

Because continued success depends on the ability to maintain good relationships with clients and potential employers for their clients, you must have good people skills; you must be able to interact tactfully and amicably with a wide variety of people, from demanding clients to busy editors. Moreover, because artists' careers have their ups and downs and production and publishing are fields with high turnover rates, you should not become complacent. You must be flexible, adaptive people, able to establish new relationships quickly and with finesse.

Exploring

If you are interested in literary management you can acquaint yourself with current trends in book publishing and with the kinds of books that particular publishing houses issue by working part-time at bookstores and libraries. If you live in a big city you may be able to get a job with a book or magazine publisher. Some literary agents also sponsor internships.

Employers

Literary agents work for established large or small agencies, although many are self-employed. Los Angeles and New York are the country's leading entertainment centers, and most agents work in either of those two cities. Some agencies have branch offices in other large U.S. cities and affiliate offices overseas, especially in London.

Starting Out

Employment within a production facility, publishing house, or entertainment center is a good beginning for agents because it provides an insider's knowledge of agents' target markets. The other optimum approach is to send resumes to any and all agencies and to be willing to start at the bottom, probably as office workers, then working up to the position of subagent, in order to learn the field.

Advancement

How far agents advance depends almost entirely on their entrepreneurial skills. Native ability alone isn't enough; successful agents must be persistent and ambitious. In addition to proving themselves to their agency superiors and clients, they must earn the trust and respect of decision-makers in the marketplace, such as publishers and producers. Once agents earn the confidence of a number of successful writers, they can strike out on their own and perhaps even establish their own agencies.

Earnings

Literary agents generally earn between $20,000 and $60,000 annually, with a rare few making hundreds of thousands of dollars a year. Because independent agents take a percentage of their clients' earnings (4 to 20 percent), their livelihoods are contingent upon the success of their clients, which is in turn contingent on the agents' ability to promote talent. Some beginning agents can go as long as a year without making any money at all, but, if at the end of that time, their clients begin to gain notice, the agents' investment of time may well pay off.

According to the Association of Authors' Representatives, New York agency assistants typically earn beginning salaries of about $20,000. Sometimes agency staffers working on commission actually can earn more money than their bosses.

Work Environment

Agents' hours are often uncertain, for in addition to fairly regular office hours, they often must meet on weekends and evenings with clients, as well as those editors with whom they are trying to build relationships. The majority of their time, however, is spent in the office on the phone. Novices can expect no more than a cubicle whereas established agents may enjoy luxurious office suites.

Established agents may travel internationally frequently to meet with clients, to scout out new talent, and find new opportunities for their talent.

Outlook

Agents work in an extremely competitive field. Most agents who attempt to go into business for themselves fail within one year. Most job openings within agencies are the result of turnover, rather than the development of new positions. There are many candidates for few positions.

For More Information

For information on the duties, responsibilities, and ethical expectations of agents, send a self-addressed #10 envelope with $0.55 postage and check or money order payable to AAR for $5 to:

Association of Authors' Representatives, Inc. (AAR)
PO Box 237201
Ansonia Station
New York, NY 10003
Tel: 212-353-3709
Web: http://www.publishersweekly.com/aar/

Magazine Editors

School Subjects	English Journalism
Personal Interests	Communication/ideas Helping/teaching
Work Environment	Primarily indoors Primarily one location
Minimum Education Level	Bachelor's degree
Salary Range	$25,000 to $50,000 to $75,000+
Certification or Licensing	None available
Outlook	Faster than the average

Overview

Magazine editors plan the contents of a magazine, assign articles and select photographs and artwork to enhance the message of the articles, and edit, organize, and sometimes rewrite the articles. They are responsible for making sure that each issue is attractive, readable, and maintains the stylistic integrity of the publication. According to the *Occupational Outlook Handbook,* of the 341,000 writers and editors employed in 1998, a third worked for newspapers, magazines, and book publishers. Many major magazines are located in large metropolitan areas, but others are published throughout the country. (See also *Editors.*)

The Job

The duties of a magazine editor are numerous, varied, and unpredictable. The editor determines each article's placement in the magazine, working closely with the sales, art, and production departments to ensure that the publication's components complement each other and are appealing and readable.

Most magazines focus on a particular topic, such as fashion, news, or sports. Current topics of interest in the magazine's specialty area dictate a magazine's content. In some cases, magazines themselves set trends, generating interest in topics that become popular. Therefore, the editor should know the latest trends in the field that the magazine represents.

Depending on the magazine's size, editors may specialize in a particular area. For example, a fashion magazine may have a beauty editor, features editor, short story editor, and fashion editor. Each editor is responsible for acquiring, proofing, rewriting, and sometimes writing articles.

After determining the magazine's contents, the editor assigns articles to writers and photographers. The editor may have a clear vision of the topic or merely a rough outline. In any case, the editor supervises the article from writing through production, assisted by copy editors, assistant editors, fact checkers, researchers, and editorial assistants. The editor also sets a department budget and negotiates contracts with freelance writers, photographers, and artists.

The magazine editor reviews each article, checking it for clarity, conciseness, and reader appeal. Frequently, the editor edits the manuscript to highlight particular items. Sometimes the magazine editor writes an editorial to stimulate discussion or mold public opinion. The editor also may write articles on topics of personal interest.

Other editorial positions at magazines include the *editor-in-chief*, who is responsible for the overall editorial course of the magazine, the *executive editor*, who controls day-to-day scheduling and operations, and the *managing editor,* who coordinates copy flow and supervises production of master pages for each issue.

Some entry-level jobs in magazine editorial departments are stepping stones to more responsible positions. *Editorial assistants* perform various tasks such as answering phones and correspondence, setting up meetings and photography shoots, checking facts, and typing manuscripts. *Editorial production assistants* assist in coordinating the layout of feature articles edited by editors and art designed by art directors to prepare the magazine for printing.

Many magazines hire *freelance writers* to write articles on an assignment or contract basis. Most freelance writers write for several different publications; some become contributing editors to one or more publications to which they contribute the bulk of their work.

Magazines also employ *researchers*, sometimes called *fact checkers*, to ensure the factual accuracy of an article's content. Researchers may be on staff or hired on a freelance basis.

Requirements

Postsecondary Training

A college degree is required for entry into this field. A degree in journalism, English, or communications is the most popular and standard degree for a magazine editor. Specialized publications prefer a degree in the magazine's specialty, such as chemistry for a chemistry magazine, and experience in writing and editing. A broad liberal arts background is important for work at any magazine.

Most colleges and universities offer specific courses in magazine design, writing, editing, and photography. Related courses might include newspaper and book editing.

Other Requirements

All entry-level positions in magazine publishing require a working knowledge of typing and word processing, plus a superior command of grammar, punctuation, and spelling. Deadlines are important, so commitment, organization, and resourcefulness are crucial.

Editing is intellectually stimulating work that may involve investigative techniques in politics, history, and business. Magazine editors must be talented wordsmiths with impeccable judgment. Their decisions about which opinions, editorials, or essays to feature may influence a large number of people.

Employers

A mid-size special-interest publication (approximately 350,000 circulation) may employ an editorial staff of 12: editor-in-chief, executive editor, managing editor, art director, four associate editors, production manager, editorial assistant, assistant to the art director, and a clerical person.

An editor for a smaller magazine hires writers, oversees production, coordinates advertising with layout, and encourages increased subscriptions. Increasing subscriptions is a key goal, as businesses review these numbers and the targeted audience when deciding how to spend advertising dollars.

Major magazines are concentrated in New York, Chicago, Los Angeles, Boston, Philadelphia, San Francisco, and Washington, DC, while professional, technical, and union publications are spread throughout the country.

Earnings

In the 1990s, salaries for experienced editors ranged from $25,000 to $43,000; editorial assistants from $20,000 to $28,000; and supervisory editors, $33,000 to $57,200 per year. Senior editors at large-circulation magazines average more than $75,000 a year. In addition, many editors supplement their salaried income by doing freelance work. According to the *Occupational Outlook Handbook*, the median annual earnings for writers and editors who worked for periodicals in 1997 were $35,900.

Full-time editors receive vacation time, medical insurance, and sick time, but freelancers must provide these for themselves.

Outlook

Magazine publishing is a dynamic industry. Magazines are launched every day of the year, although the majority fail. A recent trend in magazine publishing is focus on a special interest. There is increasing opportunity for employment at special-interest and trade magazines for those whose backgrounds complement a magazine's specialty. Association magazines offer potential employment opportunities. Internet publishing will also provide increasing job opportunities as more businesses develop online publications. Magazine editing is keenly competitive, however, and as with any career, the applicant with the most education and experience has a better chance of getting the job.

For More Information

For general and summer internship program information, contact:

Magazine Publishers of America
919 Third Avenue, 22nd Floor
New York, NY 10022
Tel: 212-872-3700
Email: infocenter@magazine.org
Web: http://www.magazine.org

Newspaper Editors

English Journalism	School Subjects
Communication/ideas Helping/teaching	Personal Interests
Primarily indoors Primarily one location	Work Environment
Bachelor's degree	Minimum Education Level
$28,500 to $30,000 to $67,000+	Salary Range
None available	Certification or Licensing
Faster than the average	Outlook

Overview

Newspaper editors assign, review, edit, rewrite, and lay out copy in a newspaper—everything except advertisements. Editors sometimes write stories or editorials that offer opinions on issues. Editors review the editorial page and copy written by staff or syndicated *columnists*. A large metropolitan daily newspaper staff may include various editors who process thousands of words into print daily. A small town weekly paper staff, however, may include only one editor, who might be both owner and star reporter. According to the *Occupational Outlook Handbook*, of the 341,000 writers and editors employed in 1998, a third worked for newspapers, magazines, and book publishers. According to *Jobs '97,* 59,000 of the 75,000 journalists worked for newspapers. Large metropolitan areas—New York, Washington, DC, Los Angeles, and Chicago—employ many editors. (See also *Editors.*)

The Job

Newspaper editors are responsible for the paper's entire news content. The news section includes features, "hard" news, and editorial commentary. Editors of a daily paper plan the contents of each day's issue, assigning articles, reviewing submissions, prioritizing stories, checking wire services, selecting illustrations, and laying out each page with the advertising space allotted.

At a large daily newspaper, an *editor-in-chief* oversees the entire editorial operation, determines its editorial policy, and reports to the publisher. The *managing editor* is responsible for day-to-day operations in an administrative capacity. *Story editors*, or *wire editors*, determine which national news agency (or wire service) stories will be used and edit them. Wire services give smaller papers, without foreign correspondents, access to international stories.

A *city editor* gathers local and sometimes state and national news. The city editor hires copy editors and reporters, hands out assignments to reporters and photographers, reviews and edits stories, confers with executive editors on story content and space availability, and gives stories to copy editors for final editing.

A newspaper may have separate desks for state, national, and foreign news, each with its own head editor. Some papers have separate *editorial page editors*. The *department editors* oversee individual features; they include business editors, fashion editors, sports editors, book section editors, entertainment editors, and more. Department heads make decisions on coverage, recommend story ideas, and make assignments. They often have backgrounds in their department's subject matter and are highly skilled at writing and editing.

The copy desk, the story's last stop, is staffed by *copy editors*, who correct spelling, grammar, and punctuation mistakes; check for readability and sense; edit for clarification; examine stories for factual accuracy; and ensure the story conforms to editorial policy. Copy editors sometimes write headlines or picture captions and may crop photos. Occasionally they find serious problems that cause them to kick stories back to the editors or the writer.

Editors, particularly copy editors, base many decisions on a style book that provides preferences in spelling, grammar, and word usage; it indicates when to use foreign spellings or English translations and the preferred system of transliteration. Some houses develop their own style books, but often they use or adapt the *Associated Press Stylebook*.

After editors approve the story's organization, coverage, writing quality, and accuracy, they turn it over to the *news editors*, who supervise article placement and determine page layout with the advertising department. News and executive editors discuss the relative priorities of major news stories. If a paper is divided into several sections, each has its own priorities.

Modern newspaper editors depend heavily on computers. Generally, a reporter types the story directly onto the computer network, providing editors with immediate access. Some editorial departments are situated remotely from printing facilities, but computers allow the printer to receive copy immediately upon approval. Today designers computerize page layout. Many columnists send their finished columns from home computers to the editorial department via modem.

Requirements

Postsecondary Training

According to *Jobs '97*, nearly 85 percent of first-time journalists had journalism or mass communications degrees. Newspapers hired 75 percent of their staffs from other newspapers or media, 25 percent from colleges; 78 percent worked at college newspapers, 83 percent as interns.

Prospective editors should find a school with strong journalism and communications programs. Many require two years of liberal arts studies before journalism study. Journalism courses include reporting, writing, and editing; press law and ethics; journalism history; and photojournalism. Advanced classes include feature writing, investigative reporting, and graphics. Some schools offer internships for credit.

Newspapers look closely at extracurricular activities, emphasizing internships, school newspaper and freelance writing and editing, and part-time newspaper work (stringing). Typing, computer skills, and knowledge of printing are helpful.

Employers

Generally there is employment for editors in every city or town, as most towns have at least one newspaper. As the population multiplies, so do the opportunities. In large metropolitan areas, there may be one or two dailies, several general interest weeklies, ethnic and other special-interest weeklies or monthlies, trade newspapers, and daily and weekly community and suburban newspapers, most with managing and department editors.

Earnings

Newspaper editors' salaries vary from small to large communities, but newspaper people generally are well compensated. Other factors affecting compensation include quality of education and previous experience, job level, and the newspaper's circulation. Large metropolitan dailies offer higher paying jobs, while outlying weekly papers pay less. According to the *Occupational Outlook Handbook*, beginning writers and editorial assistants averaged $28,500 annually while those with five or more years of experience earned more than $30,000. Senior editors at large newspapers earned more than $76,000 annually. Salary ranges and benefits for most nonmanagerial editorial workers, including editors and reporters, on many newspapers are negotiated by the Newspaper Guild.

Outlook

According to the *Occupational Outlook Handbook*, employment for editors and writers, while highly competitive, should grow faster than the average through 2008. Opportunities will be better on small daily and weekly newspapers, where the pay is lower. Some publications hire freelance editors to support reduced full-time staffs. And as experienced editors leave the workforce or move to other fields, job openings will occur.

For More Information

ASNE helps editors maintain the highest standards of quality, improve their craft, and better serve their communities. It preserves and promotes core journalistic values.

American Society of Newspaper Editors (ASNE)
11690B Sunrise Valley Drive
Reston, VA 20191-1409
Tel: 703-453-1122
Email: asne@asne.org
Web: http://www.asne.org

Founded in 1958 by The Wall Street Journal *to improve the quality of journalism education, this organization offers internships, scholarships, and literature for college students. For information on how to receive a copy of* The Journalist's Road to Success, *which lists schools offering degrees in news-editorial and financial aid to those interested in print journalism, contact:*

Dow Jones Newspaper Fund
PO Box 300
Princeton, NJ 08543-0300
Tel: 609-452-2820
Email: newsfund@wsj.dowjones.com
Web: http://www.dj.com/newsfund

To receive a free copy of Newspaper: What's in It for Me? *write:*

Newspaper Careers Project
Fulfillment Department, NAA Foundation
11600 Sunrise Valley Drive
Reston, VA 22091

This trade association for African-American-owned newspapers has a foundation that offers a scholarship and internship program for inner-city high school juniors.

National Newspaper Publishers Association
3200 13th Street, NW
Washington, DC 20010
Tel: 202-588-8764
Email: nnpadc@nnpa.org
Web: http://www.nnpa.org

This organization for journalists has campus and online chapters.

Society of Professional Journalists
16 South Jackson Street
Greencastle, IN 46135-1514
Tel: 765-653-3333
Email: spj@link2000.net
Web: http://spj.org/spjhome.htm

Photographers

	School Subjects
Art Chemistry	
	Personal Skills
Artistic Communication/ideas	
	Work Environment
Indoors and outdoors Primarily multiple locations	
	Minimum Education Level
Some postsecondary training	
	Salary Range
$16,500 to $30,700 to $38,900+	
	Certification or Licensing
None available	
	Outlook
Little change or more slowly than the average	

Overview

Photographers take and sometimes develop and print pictures of people, places, objects, and events, using a variety of cameras and photographic equipment. They work in publishing, advertising, public relations, science, and business, as well as provide personal photographic services. They may also work as fine artists.

History

The word photograph means, literally, "to write with light." Although the art of photography goes back only about 150 years, the two Greek words that were chosen and combined to refer to this skill quite accurately describe what it does.

The discoveries that led eventually to photography began early in the 18th century when a German scientist, Dr. Johann H. Schultze, experimented with the action of light on certain chemicals. He found that when these chemicals were covered by dark paper they did not change color, but when they were exposed to sunlight, they darkened. A French painter named Louis Daguerre (1787-1851) became the first photographer in 1839, when he perfected the process of using silver-iodide-coated plates inside a small box. He then developed the plates by means of mercury vapor. The daguerreotype, as these early photographs came to be known, took minutes to expose and the developing process was directly to the plate. There were no prints made.

Although the daguerreotype was the sensation of its day, it was not until George Eastman (1854-1932) invented a simple camera and flexible roll film that photography began to come into widespread use in the late 1800s. With exposure to the negative, light-sensitive paper was used to make positive multiple copies of the image.

The Job

Photography is both an artistic and technical occupation. There are many variables in the process that a knowledgable photographer can manipulate to produce a precise documentation or a work of fine art. First, photographers know how to use cameras and can adjust focus, shutter speeds, aperture, lenses, and filters. They know about the types and speeds of films. Photographers know about light and shadow, how to use available light and how to set up artificial lighting to achieve desired effects.

Some photographers send their film to laboratories, but some develop their own negatives and make their own prints. These processes require knowledge about chemicals such as developers and fixers and how to use enlarging equipment. They are familiar with the large variety of papers available for printing photographs. Most photographers continually experiment with photographic processes to improve their technical proficiency or to bend the rules to create special effects.

Digital photography is a relatively new development. Film is replaced by microchips which record pictures in digital format. They can then be downloaded onto a computer's hard drive and the photographer uses special software to manipulate the images on screen. Digital photography is used primarily for electronic publishing and advertising.

Photographers usually specialize in one of several areas: portraiture, commercial and advertising photography, photojournalism, fine art, educational photography, or scientific photography. There are subspecialties within in each of these categories. A scientific photographer, for example, may specialize in aerial or underwater photography. A commercial photographer may specialize in food or fashion photography.

Some photographers write for trade and technical journals, teach photography in schools and colleges, act as representatives of photographic equipment manufacturers, sell photographic equipment and supplies, produce documentary films, or do freelance work.

Requirements

High School

High school students should take art classes and photography classes if available. Chemistry is useful for understanding developing and printing processes. You can learn about photo manipulation software and digital photography in computer classes, and business classes will help if you are considering a freelance career.

Postsecondary Training

Formal educational requirements depend upon the nature of the photographer's specialty. For instance, photographic work in scientific and engineering research generally requires an engineering background with a degree from a recognized college or institute.

A college education is not required to become a photographer, although college training probably offers the most promising assurance of success in fields such as industrial, news, or scientific photography. Currently, 103 community and junior colleges offer associate degrees in photography, more than 160 colleges and universities offer bachelor's degrees, and 38 offer master's degrees. Many of these schools offer courses in cinematography, although very few have programs leading to a degree in this specialty. Many men and women, however, become photographers with no formal education beyond high school.

Prospective photographers should have a broad technical understanding of photography plus as much practical experience with cameras as possible. Take many different kinds of photographs with a variety of cameras and subjects. Learn how to develop photographs and, if possible, build your own darkroom or rent one. Experience in picture composition, cropping prints (cutting to desired size), enlarging, and retouching are all valuable.

Other Requirements

Students who hope to become photographers should possess manual dexterity, good eyesight and color vision, and artistic ability. You need an eye for form and line, an appreciation of light and shadow, and the ability to use imaginative and creative approaches to photographs or film, especially in commercial work. In addition, you should be patient and accurate and enjoy working with detail.

Self-employed, or freelance, photographers need good business skills. They must be able to manage their own studios, including hiring and managing photographic assistants and other employees, keeping records, and maintaining photographic and business files. Marketing and sales skills are also important to a successful freelance photography business.

Exploring

Photography is a field that almost every person with a camera can explore. Students can join high school camera clubs, yearbook or newspaper staffs, photography contests, and community hobby groups to gain experience. Students also may seek a part-time or summer job in a camera shop or work as a developer in a laboratory or processing center.

Employers

About 161,000 photographers and camera operators were employed in 1998. About half were salaried employees; the rest were self-employed. Most jobs for photographers are provided by photographic or commercial art studios; other employers include newspapers and magazines, radio and TV broadcasting, government agencies, and manufacturing firms. Colleges, universities, and other educational institutions employ photographers to prepare promotional and educational materials.

Starting Out

Some photographers enter the field as apprentices, trainees, or assistants. As a trainee, you may work in a darkroom, camera shop, or developing laboratory. You may move lights and arrange backgrounds for a commercial or portrait photographer or motion picture photographer. You may spend many months learning this kind of work before you move into a job behind a camera.

In many large cities, there are schools of photography, which may be a good way to start in the field. A press photographer may work for one of the many newspapers and magazines published in the United States and abroad. Some employers require a probationary period of 30 to 90 days before a new employee attains full job security. On publications where there is a full Newspaper Guild shop, a photographer will be required to join the guild.

Some go into business for themselves as soon as they have finished their formal education. Setting up a studio may not require a large capital outlay, but beginners may find that success does not come easily.

Advancement

Because photography is such a diversified field, there is no usual way in which to get ahead. Those who begin by working for someone else may advance to owning their own businesses. Commercial photographers may gain prestige as more of their pictures are placed in well-known trade journals or popular magazines. Press photographers may advance in salary and the kinds of important news stories assigned to them. A few photographers may become celebrities in their own right by making contributions to medical science, engineering science, or natural or physical science.

Earnings

The earnings of photographers in private industry vary according to the level of responsibility. In the 1990s, those who handle routine work earned an average of about $21,000 a year. Photographers who do difficult or challenging work earn approximately $37,200 a year.

In 1998, photographers working for newspapers that had contracts with the Newspaper Guild earned a median salary of about $24,100 a year. Most earn between $16,500 and $22,500, with the top 10 percent receiving $26,500 or more. Experienced newspaper photographers earn a median of $30,700 a year; most earn from $26,300 to $35,700 a year. The top 10 percent of experienced newspaper photographers earn in excess of $38,900.

Photographers in government service earn an average salary of about $29,500 a year. Self-employed photographers often earn more than salaried photographers, but their earnings depend on general business conditions. In addition, self-employed photographers do not have the benefits that a company provides its employees.

Photographers who combine scientific training and photographic expertise, as do scientific photographers, usually start at higher salaries than other photographers. They also usually receive consistently larger advances in salary than do others, so that their income, both as beginners and as experienced photographers, place them well above the average in their field. Photographers in salaried jobs usually receive benefits such as paid holidays, vacations, and sick leave and medical insurance.

Work Environment

Work conditions vary based on the job and employer. Many photographers work a 35- to 40-hour workweek, but freelancers and news photographers often put in long, irregular hours. Commercial and portrait photographers work in comfortable surroundings. Photojournalists seldom are assured physical comfort in their work and may in fact face danger when covering stories on natural disasters or military conflicts. Some photographers work in research laboratory settings; others work on aircraft; and still others work underwater. For some photographers, conditions change from day to day. One day, they may be photographing a hot and dusty rodeo; the next they may be taking pictures of a dog sled race in Alaska.

In general, photographers work under pressure to meet deadlines and satisfy customers. Freelance photographers have the added pressure of continually seeking new clients and uncertain incomes.

For specialists in fields such as fashion photography, breaking into the field may take years. Working as another photographer's assistant is physically demanding when carrying equipment is required.

For freelance photographers, the cost of equipment can be quite expensive, with no assurance that the money spent will be recouped through income from future assignments. Freelancers in travel-related photography, such as travel and tourism, and photojournalism, have the added cost of transportation and accommodations. For all photographers, flexibility is a major asset.

Outlook

Employment of photographers will increase more slowly than the average for all occupations through 2008, according to the *Occupational Outlook Handbook*. The demand for new images should remain strong in education, communication, entertainment, marketing, and research. As more newspapers and magazines turn to electronic publishing, it will increase the need for photographs.

Photography is a highly competitive field. There are far more photographers than positions available. Only those who are extremely talented and highly skilled can support themselves as self-employed photographers. Many photographers take pictures as a sideline while working another job.

For More Information

The ASMP promotes the rights of photographers, educates its members in business practices, and promotes high standards of ethics.

American Society of Media Photographers (ASMP)
150 North Second Street
Philadelphia, PA 19106
Tel: 215-451-2767
Web: http://www.asmp.org

The NPPA maintains a job bank, provides educational information, and makes insurance available to its members. It also publishes News Photographer *magazine.*

National Press Photographers Association (NPPA)
3200 Croasdaile Drive, Suite 306
Durham, NC 27705
Tel: 800-289-6772
Email: nppa@mindspring.com
Web: http://metalab.unc.edu/nppa/

The PPA provides training, publishes its own magazine, and offers various services for its members.

Professional Photographers of America (PPA)
229 Peachtree Street, NE, # 2200
Atlanta, GA 30303-2206
Tel: 800-786-6277
Email: csc@ppa.com
Web: http://www.ppa-world.org

Prepress Workers

School Subjects Computer science Mathematics Technical/Shop	
Personal Skills Artistic Technical/scientific	
Work Environment Primarily indoors Primarily one location	
Minimum Education Level High school diploma	
Salary Range $11,000 to $25,000 to $60,000+	
Certification or Licensing None available	
Outlook Decline	

Overview

Prepress workers handle the first stage in the printing process. Prepress is where a printed product is visually conceived and prepared for the printing press. This initial phase of production involves multiple steps, including creating pages from text and graphics and making printing plates. With the introduction of desktop publishing and other computer technology, the prepress process has changed dramatically over the past decade. Computerized processes have replaced many of the traditional processes, eliminating a number of prepress jobs but opening up new opportunities as well.

According to the U.S. Bureau of Labor Statistics, prepress jobs employed more than 135,000 people in 1998. Most of these jobs were with commercial printing companies and newspapers. Other jobs are with prepress service bureaus—companies that deal exclusively with prepress work.

History

The history of modern printing began with the invention of movable type in the 15th century. For several centuries before that, books had been printed from carved wooden blocks or laboriously copied by hand. These painstaking methods of production were so expensive that books were chained to prevent theft.

In the 1440s, Johannes Gutenberg invented a form of metal type that could be used over and over. The first known book to be printed with this movable type was a Bible in 1455—the now-famous Gutenberg Bible. Gutenberg's revolutionary new type greatly reduced the time and cost involved in printing, and books soon became plentiful.

Ottmar Mergenthaler, a German immigrant to the United States, invented the Linotype machine in 1886. Linotype allowed the typesetter to set type from a keyboard that used a mechanical device to set letters in place. Before this, printers were setting type by hand, one letter at a time, picking up each letter individually from their typecases as they had been doing for more than 400 years. At about the same time, Tolbert Lanston invented the Monotype machine, which also had a keyboard but set the type as individual letters. These inventions allowed compositors to set type much faster and more efficiently.

With these machines, newspapers advanced from the small two-page weeklies of the 1700s to the huge editions of today's metropolitan dailies. The volume of other periodicals, advertisements, books, and other printed matter also proliferated.

In the 1950s, a new system called photocomposition was introduced into commercial typesetting operations. In this system, typesetting machines used photographic images of letters, which were projected onto a photosensitive surface to compose pages. Instructions to the typesetting machine about which letters to project and where to project them were fed in through a punched-paper or magnetic tape, which was, in turn, created by an operator at a keyboard.

Most recently, typesetting has come into the home and office in the form of desktop publishing. This process has revolutionized the industry by enabling companies and individuals to do their own type composition and graphic design work.

The Job

Prepress work involves a variety of tasks, most of which are now computer-based. The prepress process is typically broken down into the following areas of responsibility: compositor and typesetter, paste-up worker, desktop publishing specialist, pre-flight technician, output technician, scanner operator, camera operator, lithographic artist, film stripper, and platemaker.

Compositors and *typesetters* are responsible for setting up and arranging type by hand or by computer into galleys for printing. This is done using "cold type" technology (as opposed to the old "hot type" method, which involved using molten lead to create letters and lines of text). A common method is phototypesetting, in which type is entered into a computer and output on photographic film or paper. Typesetting in its traditional sense requires a *paste-up worker* to then position illustrations and lay out columns of type. This manual process is quickly being phased out by desktop publishing.

Most often today, desktop publishing is the first step in the production process. The *desktop publisher* designs and lays out text and graphics on a personal computer according to the specifications of the job. This involves sizing text, setting column widths, and arranging copy with photos and other images. All elements of the piece are displayed on the computer screen and manipulated using a keyboard and mouse. In commercial printing plants, jobs tend to come from customers on computer disk, eliminating the need for initial desktop publishing work on the part of the printing company.

The entire electronic file is reviewed by the *pre-flight technician* to ensure that all of its elements are properly formatted and set up. At small print shops—which account for the majority of the printing industry—a *job printer* is often the person in charge of typesetting, page layout, proofing copy, and fixing problems with files.

Once a file is ready, the *output technician* transmits it through an imagesetter onto paper, film, or directly to a plate. The latter method is called digital imaging, and it bypasses the film stage altogether. Direct-to-plate technology has been adopted by only a small percentage of printing companies nationwide, but it is expected to be universal within the next decade.

If a file is output onto paper or provided camera-ready, the *camera operator* photographs the material and develops film negatives, either by hand or by machine. Because the bulk of commercial printing today is done using lithography, most camera operators can also be called *lithographic photographers*.

Often it is necessary to make corrections, change or reshape images, or lighten or darken the film negatives. This is the job of the *lithographic artist*, who, depending on the area of specialty, might have the title *dot etcher*, *retoucher*, or *letterer*. This film retouching work is highly specialized and is all done by hand using chemicals, dyes, and special tools.

The *film stripper* is the person who cuts film negatives to the proper size and arranges them onto large sheets called flats. The pieces are taped into place so that they are in proper position for the plate to be made.

The *platemaker*—also called a *lithographer* because of the process used in most commercial plants—creates the printing plates. This is done using a photographic process. The film is laid on top of a thin metal plate treated with a light-sensitive chemical. It is exposed to ultraviolet light, which "burns" the positive image into the plate. Those areas are then chemically treated so that when ink is applied to the plate, it adheres to the images to be printed and is repelled by the non-printing areas.

Lithography work traditionally involved sketching designs on stone, clay, or glass. Some of these older methods are still used for specialized purposes, but the predominant method today is the one previously described, which is used in offset printing. In offset printing, a series of cylinders are used to transfer ink from the chemically treated plate onto a rubber cylinder (called a blanket), then onto the paper. The printing plate never touches the paper but is "offset" by the rubber blanket.

If photos and art are not provided electronically, the *scanner operator* scans them using a high-resolution drum or flatbed scanner. In the scanning process, the continuous color tone of the original image is interpreted electronically and converted into a combination of the four primary colors used in printing: cyan (blue), magenta, yellow, and black—commonly called CMYK. A screening process separates the image into the four colors, each of which is represented by a series of dots called a halftone. These halftones are recorded to film from which printing plates are made. During the printing process, ink applied to each of the plates combines on paper to recreate the color of the original image.

Requirements

Educational requirements for prepress workers vary according to the area of responsibility, but all require at least a high school diploma, and most call for a strong command of computers.

Whereas prepress areas used to be typesetting and hand-composition operations run by people skilled in particular crafts, they are now predominantly computer-based. Workers are no longer quite as specialized and generally are competent in a variety of tasks. Thus, one of the most important criteria for prepress workers today is a solid base of computer knowledge, ideally in programs and processes related to graphic design and prepress work.

High School

Young people interested in the field are advised to take courses in computer science, mathematics, and electronics.

Postsecondary Training

The more traditional jobs, like camera operator, film stripper, lithographic artist, and platemaker, require longer, more specialized preparation. This might involve an apprenticeship or a two-year associate's degree. But these jobs now are on the decline as they are replaced by computerized processes.

Postsecondary education is strongly encouraged for most prepress positions and a requirement for some jobs, including any managerial role. Graphic arts programs are offered by community and junior colleges as well as four-year colleges and universities. Postsecondary programs in printing technology are also available.

Any programs or courses that give students exposure to the printing field will be an asset. Courses in printing are often available at vocational-technical institutes and through printing trade associations.

Other Requirements

Prepress work requires strong communications skills, attention to detail, and the ability to perform well in a high-pressure, deadline-driven environment. Physically, prepress workers should have good manual dexterity and good eyesight and overall visual perception. Artistic skill is an advantage in nearly any prepress job.

Exploring

A summer job or internship doing basic word processing or desktop publishing is one way to get a feel for what prepress work involves. Such an opportunity could even be found through a temporary agency. Of course, a knowledge of computers and certain software will be needed.

You also can volunteer to do desktop publishing or design work for your school newspaper or yearbook. This would have the added benefit of exposing you to the actual printing process.

Employers

The U.S. Bureau of Labor Statistics reported there were over 135,000 pre-press jobs in 1998. Of these, 26,000 were desktop publishing jobs. The majority of prepress work is in firms that do commercial or business printing and in newspaper plants. Other jobs are at companies that specialize in certain aspects of the prepress process—for example, platemaking or outputting of film.

Because printing is so widespread, prepress jobs are available in almost any part of the country. However, according to the *Occupational Outlook Handbook*, prepress work is concentrated in large printing centers like New York, Chicago, Los Angeles, Philadelphia, Dallas, and Washington, DC.

Starting Out

Information on apprenticeships and training opportunities is available through state employment services and local chapters of printing industry associations.

Those who wish to start working first and learn their skills on the job should contact potential employers directly, especially if they want to work in a small nonunion print shop. Openings for trainee positions may be listed in newspaper want ads or with the state employment service. Trade school graduates may find jobs through their school's placement office. And industry association offices often run job listing services.

Advancement

Some prepress work, such as typesetting, can be learned fairly quickly; other jobs, like film stripping or platemaking, take years to master. Workers often begin as assistants and move into on-the-job training programs. Entry-level workers are trained by more experienced workers and advance according to how quickly they learn and prove themselves.

In larger companies, prepress workers can move up the ranks to take on supervisory roles. Prepress and production work is also a good starting point for people who aim to become a customer service or sales representative for a printing company.

Earnings

Pay rates vary for prepress workers, depending on their level of experience and responsibility, type of company, where they live, and whether or not they are union members. The *Occupational Outlook Handbook* reports that the median earnings of lithographers and photoengravers were $460 a week. Typesetters and compositors earned a reported $435 a week. The handbook quoted 1998 wages of $23.20 an hour for scanner operators and $19.45 an hour for film strippers. According to the book *Careers in Graphic Communications* (Graphic Arts Technical Foundation, 1998), some jobs, such as color scanner operator, pay up to $18 per hour. And high-tech color specialists, who manipulate color in a document before it goes to press, are paid in the range of $40,000 to $60,000.

Work Environment

Generally, prepress workers work in clean, quiet settings away from the noise and activity of the pressroom. Prepress areas are usually air-conditioned and roomy. Desktop publishers and others who work in front of computer terminals can risk straining their eyes, as well as their backs and necks. Film stripping and other detail-oriented work also can be tiring to the eyes. The chemicals used in platemaking can irritate the skin.

An eight-hour day is typical for most prepress jobs, but frequently workers put in more than eight hours. Prepress jobs at newspapers and financial printers often call for weekend and evening hours.

Outlook

Overall employment in the prepress portion of the printing industry is expected to decline through 2008, according to the U.S. Bureau of Labor Statistics. While it is anticipated that the demand for printed materials will increase, prepress work will not, mainly because of new innovations.

The bureau projects that almost all prepress operations will be computerized by 2008. This will phase out many of the traditional jobs that involved highly skilled hand work: film strippers, paste-up workers, photoengravers, camera operators, and platemakers.

However, the computer-oriented aspects of prepress work are another story. Desktop publishing specialists, for example, will be in heavy demand in the near future. And specialized computer skills will increasingly be needed to handle direct-to-plate and other new technology.

Given the increasing demand for rush print jobs, printing trade service companies should offer good opportunities for prepress workers. Larger companies and companies not equipped for specialized prepress work will continue to turn to these specialty shops to keep up with their workload.

For More Information

This organization offers information, services, and training related to printing, electronic prepress, electronic publishing, and other areas of the graphic arts industry.

Graphic Arts Technical Foundation
200 Deer Run Road
Sewickley, PA 15143-2600
Tel: 412-741-6860
Email: info@gatf.org
Web: http://www.gatf.org

This industry coalition serves as a clearinghouse, resource center, and coordinator of programs promoting career awareness, training, and a positive industry image. Its goal is "to attract bright young minds into the graphic communications industry."

Graphic Communications Council
1899 Preston White Drive
Reston, VA 22091
Tel: 703-648-1768
Email: edcouncil@npes.org
Web: http://www.npes.org/edcouncil/index.htm

This organization represents U.S. and Canadian workers in all craft and skill areas of the printing and publishing industries. In addition to developing cooperative relationships with employers, it also offers education and training through local union schools.

Graphic Communications International Union
1900 L Street, NW
Washington, DC 20036
Tel: 202-462-1400
Web: http://www.gciu.org

This trade association of graphic communications and graphic arts supplier companies offers economic and management information, publications, and industry reports and studies.

International Prepress Association
7200 France Avenue South, Suite 327
Edina, MN 55435
Tel: 612-896-1908
Web: http://www.ipa.org

This graphic arts trade association is a good source for genral information.

National Association of Printers and Lithographers
75 West Century Road
Paramus, NJ 07652
Tel: 201-634-9600
Email: napl@napl.org
Web: http://www.napl.org

Printing Press Operators and Assistants

School Subjects
- Computer science
- Mathematics
- Technical/Shop

Personal Skills
- Mechanical/manipulative
- Technical/scientific

Work Environment
- Primarily indoors
- Primarily one location

Minimum Education Level
- High school diploma

Salary Range
- $11,440 to $26,000 to $43,680+

Certification or Licensing
- Voluntary

Outlook
- Little change or more slowly than the average

Overview

Printing press operators and *printing press assistants* prepare, operate, and maintain printing presses. Their principal duties include installing and adjusting printing plates, loading and feeding paper, mixing inks and controlling ink flow, and ensuring the quality of the final printed piece.

According to the U.S. Bureau of Labor Statistics, there were over 253,000 printing press operators in the United States in 1998. They were mostly employed by newspaper plants and commercial and business printers.

History

The forerunners of today's modern printing presses were developed in Germany in the 15th century. They made use of the new concept of movable type, an invention generally credited to Johannes Gutenberg. Before Gutenberg's time, most books were copied by hand or printed from carved wooden blocks. Movable type used separate pieces of metal that could be easily set in place, locked into a form for printing, and then used again for another job.

The first presses consisted of two flat surfaces. Once set in place, the type was inked with a roller, and a sheet of paper was pressed against the type with a lever. Two people working together could print about 300 pages a day.

In the early 19th century, Friedrich Konig, another German, developed the first cylinder press. With a cylinder press, the paper is mounted on a large cylinder that is rolled over a flat printing surface.

The first rotary press was developed in the United States in 1865 by William Bullock. On this kind of press, the inked surface is on a revolving cylinder called a plate cylinder. The plate cylinder acts like a roller and prints onto a continuous sheet of paper (called a web) coming off a giant roll.

The speed and economy of the web press was improved by the discovery of offset printing in the early 20th century. In this process, the raised metal type used in earlier processes was substituted with a flexible plate that could be easily attached to the plate cylinder. The ink is transferred from the plate onto a rubber cylinder (called a blanket), then onto the paper. The printing plate never touches the paper but is "offset" by the rubber blanket.

Offset printing uses the process of lithography, in which the plate is chemically treated so that ink sticks only to the parts that are to be printed and is repelled by the non-print areas.

Offset lithography is the most common form of printing today and is used on both web-fed and sheet-fed presses. Web-fed presses are used for newspapers and other large-volume, lower-cost runs. The fastest web presses today can print about 150,000 complete newspapers in an hour. Sheet-fed presses, which print on single sheets of paper rather than a continuous roll, are used for smaller, higher-quality jobs.

Other forms of printing are gravure (in which depressions on an etched plate are inked and pressed to paper), flexography (a form of rotary printing using flexible rubber plates with raised image areas and fast-drying inks), and letterpress (the most traditional method, in which a plate with raised, inked images is pressed against paper).

The Job

The duties of press operators and their assistants vary according to the size of the printing plant in which they work. Generally, they are involved in all aspects of making the presses ready for a job and monitoring and operating the presses during the print run. Because most presses now are computerized, the work of press operators involves both electronic and manual processes.

In small shops, press operators usually handle all of the tasks associated with running a press, including cleaning and oiling the parts and making minor repairs. In larger shops, press operators are aided by assistants who handle most maintenance and cleanup tasks.

Once the press has been inspected and the printing plate arrives from the platemaker, the "makeready" process begins. In this stage, the operators mount the plates into place on the printing surface or cylinder. They mix and match the ink, fill the ink fountains, and adjust the ink flow and dampening systems. They also load the paper, adjust the press to the paper size, feed the paper through the cylinders and, on a web press, adjust the tension controls. When this is done, a proof sheet is run off for the customer's review.

When the proof has been approved and final adjustments have been made, the press run begins. During the run, press operators constantly check the quality of the printed sheets and make any necessary adjustments. They look to see that the print is clear and properly positioned and that ink is not offsetting (blotting) onto other sheets. If the job involves color, they make sure that the colors line up properly with the images they are assigned to (this is called registration). Operators also monitor the chemical properties of the ink and correct temperatures in the drying chamber, if the press has one.

On a web press, the feeding and tension mechanisms must be continually monitored. If the paper tears or jams, it must be rethreaded. As a roll of paper runs out, a new one must be spliced onto the old one. According to *Careers in Graphic Communications* (Graphic Arts Technical Foundation, 1998), some web presses today can print up to 50,000 feet an hour. At this rate, the press might run through a giant roll of paper every half hour. In large web printing plants, it takes an entire crew of specialized operators to oversee the process.

Most printing plants now have computerized printing presses equipped with sophisticated instrumentation. Press operators work at a control panel that monitors the printing processes and can adjust each variable automatically.

Requirements

High School

The minimum educational requirement for printing press operators and assistants is a high school diploma. Students interested in this field should take courses that offer an introduction to printing and color theory, as well as chemistry, computer science, electronics, mathematics, and physics—any course that develops mechanical and mathematical aptitude.

Postsecondary Training

Postsecondary training in a vocational-technical or graphic arts program is also recommended. And computer training is essential.

With today's rapid advances in technology, "students need all the computer knowledge they can get," advises John Smotherman, press operator and shift supervisor at Busch and Schmidt Company in Broadview, Illinois.

Certification or Licensing

The National Council for Skill Standards in Graphic Communications offers the designation of National Council Certified Operator.

Other Requirements

Strong communication skills—both verbal and written—are a must for press operators and assistants. They also must be able to work well as a team, both with each other and with others in the printing company. Any miscommunication during the printing process can be costly if it means re-running a job or any part of it. Working well under pressure is another requirement since most print jobs run on tight deadlines.

Exploring

High school is a good time to begin exploring the occupation of printing press operator. Some schools offer print shop classes, which provide the most direct exposure to this work. Working on the high school newspaper or yearbook is another way to gain a familiarity with the printing process. A delivery job with a print shop or a visit to a local printing plant will offer you the chance to see presses in action and get a feel for the environment in which press operators work. You also might consider a part-time, temporary, or summer job as a cleanup worker or press feeder in a printing plant.

Employers

There were over 253,000 press operator jobs in the United States in 1998, according to the U.S. Bureau of Labor Statistics. The bulk of these were with newspapers and commercial and business printers. Companies range from small print shops, where one or two press operators handle everything, to large corporations that employ teams of press operators to work around the clock.

Other press operator jobs are with in-plant operations—that is, in companies and organizations that do their own printing in-house.

Because printing is so geographically diverse, press operator jobs are available in almost any city or town in the country. However, according to the *Occupational Outlook Handbook*, press work is concentrated in large printing centers like New York, Chicago, Los Angeles, Philadelphia, Dallas, and Washington, DC.

Starting Out

Traditionally, press operators learned their craft through apprenticeship programs ranging from two to five years. Apprenticeships are still available, but they are being phased out by postsecondary programs in printing equipment operation offered by technical and trade schools and community and junior colleges. Information on apprenticeships is often available through state employment services and local chapters of printing industry associations.

In addition to classroom education, on-the-job training is needed. Openings for trainee positions may be listed in newspaper want ads or with the state employment service. Trade school graduates may find jobs through their school's placement office. And industry association offices often run job listing services.

Smotherman notes that many young people entering the field start out in a part-time position while still in school. "I think students should pursue all the classroom education they can, but many intricacies of the printing process, like how certain inks and papers work together, need to be learned through experience," he says.

Advancement

Most printing press operators, even those with some training, begin their careers doing entry-level work, such as loading, unloading, and cleaning the presses. In large print shops, the line of promotion is usually as follows: press helper, press assistant, press operator, press operator-in-charge, press room supervisor, superintendent.

Press operators can advance in salary and responsibility level by learning to work more complex printing equipment—for example by moving from a one-color press to a four-color press. Printing press operators should be prepared to continue their training and education throughout their careers. As printing companies upgrade their equipment and buy new, more computerized presses, retraining will be essential.

Press operators who are interested in other aspects of the printing business also may find advancement opportunities elsewhere in their company. Those with business savvy may be successful in establishing their own print shops.

Earnings

Pay rates vary for press operators, depending on their level of experience and responsibility, type of company, where they live, and whether or not they are union members. The *Occupational Outlook Handbook* reported that the median weekly earnings of press operators were about $500 in 1998. The salary ranges cited in *Careers in Graphic Communications* (Graphic Arts Technical

Foundation, 1998): minimum wage for entry-level workers to $21 an hour for veteran operators.

Work Environment

Pressrooms are well-ventilated, well-lit, and humidity-controlled. They are also noisy. Often press operators must wear ear protectors. Press work can be physically strenuous and requires a lot of standing. Press operators also have considerable contact with ink and cleaning fluids that can cause skin and eye irritation.

Working around large machines can be hazardous, so press operators must constantly observe good safety habits.

An eight-hour day is typical for most press operators, but some work longer hours. Smaller plants generally have only a day shift, but many larger plants and newspaper printers run around the clock. At these plants, like in hospitals and factories, press operator shifts are broken into day, afternoon/evening, and "graveyard" hours.

Outlook

The U.S. Department of Labor predicts that employment of press operators will grow very little through 2008 as compared to all other occupations. An increased demand for printed materials—advertising, direct mail pieces, computer software packaging, books, and magazines—will be offset by the use of larger, more efficient machines.

Newcomers to the field are likely to encounter stiff competition from experienced workers or workers who have completed retraining programs to update their skills. Opportunities are expected to be greatest for students who have completed formal apprenticeships or postsecondary training programs.

Jobs in letterpress printing will continue to decline, while opportunities are expected grow in offset lithography, gravure, and flexography printing.

"If you're not afraid of work or learning, you can do well in this industry," Smotherman says.

For More Information

For more information on the National Council Certified Operator designation, contact:

National Council for Skill Standards in Graphic Communications
408 Lafayette Center
Kennebunk, ME 04043-1800
Tel: 207-985-9898
Email: nc-skl-stds@cybertours.com

The Graphic Arts Technical Foundation (GATF) offers information, services, and training related to printing, electronic prepress, electronic publishing, and other areas of the graphic arts industry. GATF also sponsors the National Scholarship Trust Fund (NSTF) of the Graphic Arts, which awards scholarships to undergraduate and graduate students preparing to enter the field of graphic communications. (Scholarship applications may be downloaded from the GATF Web site listed below.) NSTF also publishes a directory of technical schools, colleges, and universities that offer courses in graphic communications.

Graphic Arts Technical Foundation (GAFT)
200 Deer Run Road
Sewickley, PA 15143-2600
Tel: 412-741-6860
Email: info@gatf.org
Web: http://www.gatf.org

This industry coalition serves as a clearinghouse, resource center, and coordinator of programs promoting career awareness, training, and a positive industry image. Its goal is "to attract bright young minds into the graphic communications industry."

Graphic Communications Council
1899 Preston White Drive
Reston, VA 22091
Tel: 703-264-7200
Web: http://www.npes.org/edcouncil/index.htm

This union represents U.S. and Canadian workers in all craft and skill areas of the printing and publishing industries. In addition to developing cooperative relationships with employers, the organization also offers education and training through local union schools.

Graphic Communications International Union
1900 L Street, NW
Washington, DC 20036
Tel: 202-462-1400
Web: http://www.gciu.org

This graphic arts trade association is a good source of general information.

National Association of Printing Leadership
75 West Century Road
Paramus, NJ 07652
Tel: 201-634-9600
Email: info@napl.org
Web: http://www.napl.org

Reporters

English Journalism	School Subjects
Communication/ideas Helping/teaching	Personal Skills
Indoors and outdoors Primarily multiple locations	Work Environment
Bachelor's degree	Minimum Education Level
$17,500 to $50,000 to $100,000+	Salary Range
None available	Certification or Licensing
Little change or more slowly than the average	Outlook

Overview

Reporters are the foot soldiers for newspapers, magazines, and television and radio broadcast companies. They gather and analyze information about current events and write stories for publication or for broadcasting.

History

Newspapers are primary disseminators of news in the United States. People read newspapers to learn about the current events that are shaping their society and societies around the world. Newspapers give public expression to opinion and criticism of government and societal issues, and of course, provide the public with entertaining, informative reading.

Newspapers are able to fulfill these functions because of the freedom given to the press. However, this was not always the case. The first American newspaper, published in 1690, was suppressed four days after it was published. And it was not until 1704 that the first continuous newspaper appeared.

One early newspaperman who later became a famous writer was Benjamin Franklin. Franklin worked for his brother at a Boston newspaper before publishing his own two years later in 1723 in Philadelphia.

A number of developments in the printing industry made it possible for newspapers to be printed more cheaply. In the late 19th century, new types of presses were developed to increase production, and more important, the linotype machine was invented. The linotype mechanically set the letters so that handset type was no longer necessary. This dramatically decreased the amount of prepress time needed to get a page into print. Newspapers could respond to breaking stories more quickly; late editions with breaking stories became part of the news world.

These technological advances, along with an increasing population, factored in the rapid growth of the newspaper industry in the United States. In 1776, there were only 37 newspapers in the United States. Today there are more than 1,500 daily and nearly 7,500 weekly newspapers in the country.

As newspapers grew in size and widened the scope of their coverage, it became necessary to increase the number of employees and to assign them specialized jobs. Reporters have always been the heart of newspaper staffs. However, in today's complex world, with the public hungry for news as it occurs, reporters and correspondents are involved in all media—not only newspapers, but magazines, radio, and television as well. Today, with the advent of the Internet, many newspapers are going online, causing many reporters to become active participants on the information superhighway.

The Job

Reporters collect information on newsworthy events and prepare stories for newspaper or magazine publication or for radio or television broadcast. The stories may simply provide information about local, state, or national events, or they may present opposing points of view on issues of current interest. In this latter capacity, the press plays an important role in monitoring the actions of public officials and others in positions of power.

Stories may originate as an assignment from an editor or as the result of a lead or news tip. Good reporters are always on the lookout for good story ideas. To cover a story, they gather and verify facts by interviewing people involved in or related to the event, examining documents and public records, observing events as they happen, and researching relevant background information. Reporters generally take notes or use a tape recorder as they collect information and write their stories once they return to their offices. In order to meet a deadline, they may have to telephone the stories to *rewriters*, who write or transcribe the stories for them. After the facts have been gathered and verified, the reporters transcribe their notes, organize their material, and determine what emphasis, or angle, to give the news. The story is then written to meet prescribed standards of editorial style and format.

The basic functions of reporters are to observe events objectively and impartially, record them accurately, and explain what the news means in a larger, societal context. Within this framework, there are several types of reporters.

The most basic is the news reporter. This job sometimes involves covering a beat, such as the police station, courthouse, or school system. It may involve receiving general assignments, such as a story about an unusual occurrence or an obituary of a community leader. Large daily papers may assign teams of reporters to investigate social, economic, or political events and conditions.

Many newspaper, wire service, and magazine reporters specialize in one type of story, either because they have a particular interest in the subject or because they have acquired the expertise to analyze and interpret news in that particular area. Topical reporters cover stories for a specific department, such as medicine, politics, foreign affairs, sports, consumer affairs, finance, science, business, education, labor, or religion. They sometimes write features explaining the history that has led up to certain events in the field they cover. Feature writers generally write longer, broader stories than news reporters, usually on more upbeat subjects, such as fashion, art, theater, travel, and social events. They may write about trends, for example, or profile local celebrities. Editorial writers and syndicated news columnists present viewpoints that, although based on a thorough knowledge, are opinions on topics of popular interest. Columnists write under a byline and usually specialize in a particular subject, such as politics or government activities. Critics review restaurants, books, works of art, movies, plays, musical performances, and other cultural events.

Specializing allows reporters to focus their efforts, talent, and knowledge on one area of expertise. It also allows them more opportunities to develop deeper relationships with contacts and sources necessary to gain access to the news.

Correspondents report events in locations distant from their home offices. They may report news by mail, telephone, fax, or computer from rural areas, large cities throughout the United States, or countries. Many large newspapers, magazines, and broadcast companies have one correspondent who is responsible for covering all the news for the foreign city or country where they are based.

Reporters on small or weekly newspapers not only cover all aspects of the news in their communities, but they also may take photographs, write editorials and headlines, lay out pages, edit wire-service copy, and help with general office work. Television reporters may have to be photogenic as well as talented and resourceful: they may at times present live reports, filmed by a mobile camera unit at the scene where the news originates, or they may tape interviews and narration for later broadcast.

Requirements

High School

High school courses that provide a firm foundation for a career as reporter include English, journalism, social studies, speech, typing, and computer science.

Postsecondary Training

A bachelor's degree is essential for aspiring reporters. Graduate degrees give students a great advantage over those entering the field with lesser degrees. Most editors prefer applicants with degrees in journalism because their studies include liberal arts courses as well as professional training in journalism. Some editors consider it sufficient for a reporter to have a good general education from a liberal arts college. Others prefer applicants with an undergraduate degree in liberal arts and a master's degree in journalism. The great majority of journalism graduates hired today by newspapers, wire services, and magazines have majored specifically in news-editorial journalism.

More than 400 colleges offer programs in journalism leading to a bachelor's degree. In these schools, around three-fourths of a student's time is devoted to a liberal education and one-fourth to the professional study of journalism, with required courses such as introductory mass media, basic reporting and copy editing, history of journalism, and press law and ethics. Students are encouraged to select other journalism courses according to their specific interests.

Journalism courses and programs are also offered by more than 350 community and junior colleges. Graduates of these programs are prepared to go to work directly as general assignment reporters, but they may encounter difficulty when competing with graduates of four-year programs. Credit earned in community and junior colleges may be transferable to four-year programs in journalism at other colleges and universities. Journalism training may also be obtained in the armed forces. Names and addresses of newspapers and a list of journalism schools and departments are published in the *Editor and Publisher International Year Book*, which is available for reference in most public libraries and newspaper offices.

A master's degree in journalism may be earned at more than 157 schools, and a doctorate at about 32 schools. Graduate degrees may prepare students specifically for careers in news or as journalism teachers, researchers, and theorists or for jobs in advertising or public relations.

A reporter's liberal arts training should include courses in English (with an emphasis on writing), sociology, political science, economics, history, psychology, business, speech, and computer science. Knowledge of foreign languages is also useful. To be a reporter in a specialized field, such as science or finance, requires concentrated course work in that area.

Other Requirements

A crucial requirement for reporters is typing skill. Reporters type their stories using word processing programs. Although not essential, a knowledge of shorthand or speedwriting makes note taking easier, and an acquaintance with news photography is an asset.

Reporters must be inquisitive, aggressive, persistent, and detail-oriented. They must enjoy interaction with people of various races, cultures, religions, economic levels, and social statuses.

Exploring

You can explore a career as a reporter in a number of ways. You can talk to reporters and editors at local newspapers and radio and TV stations. You can interview the admissions counselor at the school of journalism closest to your home.

In addition to taking courses in English, journalism, social studies, speech, computer science, and typing, high school students can acquire practical experience by working on school newspapers or on a church, synagogue, or mosque newsletter. Part-time and summer jobs on newspapers provide invaluable experience to the aspiring reporter.

College students can develop their reporting skills in the laboratory courses or workshops that are part of the journalism curriculum. College students might also accept jobs as campus correspondents for selected newspapers. People who work as part-time reporters covering news in a particular area of a community are known as stringers and are paid only for those stories that are printed.

More than 3,000 journalism scholarships, fellowships, and assistantships are offered by universities, newspapers, foundations, and professional organizations to college students. Many newspapers and magazines offer summer internships to journalism students to provide them with practical experience in a variety of basic reporting and editing duties. Students who successfully complete internships are usually placed in jobs more quickly upon graduation than those without such experience.

Employers

Of the approximately 67,000 reporters and correspondents employed in 1998, about 60 percent worked for newspapers of all sizes. The rest were employed by wire services, magazines, and radio and television broadcasting companies.

Starting Out

Jobs in this field may be obtained through college placement offices or by applying directly to the personnel departments of individual employers. Applicants with some practical experience will have an advantage; they should be prepared to present a portfolio of material they wrote as volunteer or part-time reporters or other writing samples.

Most journalism school graduates start out as general assignment reporters or copy editors for small publications. A few outstanding journalism graduates may be hired by large city newspapers or national magazines. They are trained on the job. But they are the exception, as large employers usually require several years' experience. As a rule, novice reporters cover routine assignments, such as reporting on civic and club meetings, writing obituaries, or summarizing speeches. As reporters become more skilled, they are assigned to more important events or to a regular beat, or they may specialize in a particular field.

Advancement

Reporters may advance by moving to larger newspapers or press services, but competition for such positions is unusually keen. Many highly qualified reporters apply for these jobs every year.

A select number of reporters eventually become columnists, correspondents, editorial writers, editors, or top executives. These important and influential positions represent the top of the field, and competition is strong for them.

Many reporters transfer the contacts and knowledge developed in newspaper reporting to related fields, such as public relations, advertising, or preparing copy for radio and television news programs.

Earnings

There are great variations in the earnings of reporters. Salaries are related to experience, kind of employer for which the reporter works, geographical location, and whether the reporter is covered by a contract negotiated by the Newspaper Guild.

In the late 1990s, reporters on daily newspapers having Newspaper Guild contracts received starting salaries that ranged from about $10,000 in Battle Creek, Michigan, to $68,000 in New York City. The average starting salary was about $25,000. Reporters with between two and six years of experience earned salaries that ranged from $18,000 to $70,000. Some top reporters on big city dailies earned even more, on the basis of merit or seniority.

Reporters who worked in radio earned an average salary of $15,000 a year. Some who worked for stations in large cities earned up to $36,000. Reporters who worked in television earned between $17,500 and $55,000, depending on the size of the station. High-profile columnists and newscasters working for prestigious papers or network television stations earned over $100,000 a year.

Work Environment

Reporters work under a great deal of pressure in settings that differ from the typical business office. Their jobs generally require a five-day, 35- to 40-hour week, but overtime and irregular schedules are very common. Reporters employed by morning papers start work in the late afternoon and finish around midnight, while those on afternoon or evening papers start early in the morning and work until early or midafternoon. Foreign correspondents often work late at night to send the news to their papers in time to meet printing deadlines.

The day of the smoky, ink-stained newsroom has passed, but newspaper offices are still hectic places. Reporters have to work amid the clatter of computer keyboards and other machines, loud voices engaged in telephone conversations, and the bustle created by people hurrying about. An atmosphere of excitement and bustle prevails, especially as press deadlines approach.

Travel is often required in this occupation, and some assignments may be dangerous, such as covering wars, political uprisings, fires, floods, and other events of a volatile nature.

Outlook

Employment for reporters and correspondents through 2008 is expected to grow somewhat slower than the average for all occupations. According to Bureau of Labor Statistics projections, the number of employed reporters and correspondents is projected to decline by about 3 percent within the next several years. While the number of self-employed reporters and correspondents is expected to grow about 9 percent by 2008 (and magazine workers by about 7 percent), newpaper jobs are expected to decrease by about 9 percent. Jobs in other communications settings also are projected to decline slightly.

Because of an increase in the number of small community and suburban daily and weekly newspapers, opportunities will be best for journalism graduates who are willing to relocate and accept relatively low starting salaries. With experience, reporters on these small papers can move up to editing positions or may choose to transfer to reporting jobs on larger newspapers or magazines.

Openings will be limited on big city dailies. While individual papers may enlarge their reporting staffs, little or no change is expected in the total number of these newspapers. Applicants will face strong competition for jobs on large metropolitan newspapers. Experience is a definite requirement, which rules out most new graduates unless they possess credentials in an area for which the publication has a pressing need. Occasionally, a beginner can use contacts and experience gained through internship programs and summer jobs to obtain a reporting job immediately after graduation.

A significant number of jobs will be provided by magazines and in radio and television broadcasting, but the major news magazines and larger broadcasting stations generally prefer experienced reporters. For beginning correspondents, small stations with local news broadcasts will continue to replace staff who move on to larger stations or leave the business. Network hiring has been cut drastically in the past few years and will probably continue to decline.

Overall, the prospects are best for graduates who have majored in news-editorial journalism and completed an internship while in school. The top graduates in an accredited program will have a great advantage, as will talented *technical writers*. Small newspapers prefer to hire beginning reporters who are acquainted with the community and are willing to help with photography and other aspects of production. Without at least a bachelor's degree in journalism, applicants will find it increasingly difficult to obtain even an entry-level position.

Those with doctorates and practical reporting experience may find teaching positions at four-year colleges and universities, while highly qualified reporters with master's degrees may obtain employment in journalism departments of community and junior colleges.

Poor economic conditions do not drastically affect the employment of reporters and correspondents. Their numbers are not severely cut back even during a downturn; instead, employers forced to reduce expenditures will suspend new hiring.

For More Information

This organization provides general educational information on all areas of journalism (newspapers, magazines, television, and radio). A Look at Careers in Journalism and Mass Communications, 12 pages, describes the various career opportunities in the field.

> **Association for Education in Journalism and Mass Communication**
> 234 Outlet Pointe Boulevard
> Columbia, SC 29210-5667
> Tel: 803-798-0271
> Email: aejmchq@aol.com

To receive a copy of The Journalist's Road to Success, which lists schools offering degrees in news-editorial and financial aid to those interested in print journalism, contact:

> **Dow Jones Newspaper Fund**
> PO Box 300
> Princeton, NJ 08543-0300
> Tel: 609-452-2820
> Email: newsfund@plink.geis.com
> Web: http://www.dj.com/newsfund

To receive a free copy of Newspaper: What's in It for Me? write:

> **Newspaper Careers Project**
> Fulfillment Department NAA Foundation
> 11600 Sunrise Valley Drive
> Reston, VA 22091

Science and Medical Writers

English **Journalism**	School Subjects
Communication/ideas **Technical/scientific**	Personal Skills
Bachelor's degree	Minimum Education Level
$37,000 to $47,500 to $59,000	Salary Range
Voluntary	Certification or Licensing
Faster than the average	Outlook

Overview

Science and medical writers translate technical medical and scientific information so it can be disseminated to the general public and professionals in the field. Science and medical writers are involved with researching, interpreting, writing, and editing scientific and medical information. Their work often appears in books, technical studies and reports, magazine and trade journal articles, newspapers, company newsletters, on Web sites, and may be used for radio and television broadcasts.

History

The skill of writing has existed for thousands of years. Papyrus fragments with writing by ancient Egyptians date from about 3000 BC, and archaeological findings show that the Chinese had developed books by about 1300 BC. A number of technical obstacles had to be overcome before printing and the writing profession progressed.

The modern publishing age began in the 18th century. Printing became mechanized, and the novel, magazine, and newspaper developed. Developments in the printing trades, photoengraving, retailing, and the availability of capital produced a boom in newspapers and magazines in the 19th century. Further mechanization in the printing field, such as the use of the Linotype machine, high-speed rotary presses, and special color reproduction processes, set the stage for still further growth in the book, newspaper, and magazine industry.

In addition to the print media, the broadcasting industry has contributed to the development of the professional writer. Film, radio, and television are sources of entertainment, information, and education that provide employment for thousands of writers. Today, the computer industry, and the Internet and its proliferation of Web sites, have also created the need for more writers.

As our world has become more complex and people are seeking even more information, the professional writer has become increasingly important. And, as medicine and science are taking giant steps forward and discoveries are being made every day that impact our lives, skilled science and medical writers are needed to document these changes and disseminate the information.

The Job

Science or medical writers usually write about subjects related to these fields. Because the medical and scientific subject areas may sometimes overlap, writers often find that they do science writing as well as medical writing. For instance a medical writer might write about a scientific study that has an impact on the medical field.

Medical and science writing may be targeted for the printed page, the broadcast media, or the Web. It can be specific to one product and one type of writing, such as writing medical information and consumer publications for a specific drug line produced by a pharmaceutical company. Research facilities hire writers to edit reports or write about their scientific or medical studies. Writers who are public information officers write press releases that inform the public about the latest scientific or medical research findings. An educational publisher uses writers to write or edit educational materials for the medical profession. Science and medical writers also write online articles or interactive courses that are distributed over the Internet.

According to Barbara Gastel, M.D., coordinator of the Master of Science Program in Science and Technology Journalism at Texas A&M, many science and technology-related industries are using specialized writers to communicate complex subjects to the public. "In addition," she says, "opportunities exist in the popular media. Newspapers, radio, TV, and the Web have writers who specialize in covering medical and scientific subjects."

Science and medical writers usually write for the general public. They translate high-tech information into articles and reports that can be understood by the general public and the media. Good writers who cover the subjects thoroughly have inquisitive minds and enjoy looking for additional information that might add to their articles. They research the topic to gain a thorough understanding of the subject matter. This may require hours of research on the Internet, or in corporate, university, or public libraries. Writers always need good background information regarding a subject before they can write about it.

In order to get the information required, writers may interview professionals such as doctors, pharmacists, scientists, engineers, managers, and others familiar with the subject. Writers must know how to present the information so it can be understood. This requires knowing the audience and how to reach them. For example, an article may need graphs, photos, or historical facts. Writers sometimes enlist the help of technical or medical illustrators or engineers in order to add a visual dimension to their work.

For example, if reporting on a new heart surgery procedure that will soon be available to the public, writers may need to illustrate how that surgery is performed and what areas of the heart are affected. They may give a basic overview of how the healthy heart works, show a diseased heart in comparison, and report on how this surgery can help the patient. The public will also want to know how many people are affected by this disease, what the symptoms are, how many procedures have been done successfully, where they were performed, what the recovery time is, and if there are any complications. In addition, interviews with doctors and patients add a personal touch to the story.

Broadcast media need short, precise articles that can be transmitted in a specific time allotment. Writers usually need to work quickly because news-related stores are often deadline oriented. Because science and medicine can be so complex, science and medical writers also need to help the audience understand and evaluate the information. Writing for the Web encompasses most journalistic guidelines including time constraints and sometimes space constraints.

Some science and medical writers specialize in their subject matter. For instance, a medical writer may write only about heart disease and earn a reputation as the best writer in that subject area. Science writers may limit their writing or research to environmental science subjects, or may be even more specific and focus only on air pollution issues.

According to Jeanie Davis, president of the Southeast Chapter of the American Medical Writers Association, "Medical writing can take several different avenues. You may be a consumer medical writer, write technical medical research, or write about health care issues. Some choose to be medical editors and edit reports written by researchers. Sometimes this medical research must be translated into reports and news releases that the public can understand. Today many writers write for the Web." Davis adds, "It is a very dynamic profession, always changing."

Dr. Gastel says, "This career can have various appeals. People can combine their interest in science or medicine with their love of writing. It is a good field for a generalist who likes science and doesn't want to be tied to research in one area. Plus," she adds, "it is always fun to get things published."

Some writers may choose to be freelance writers either on a full- or part-time basis, or to supplement other jobs. *Freelance science and medical writers* are self-employed writers who work with small and large companies, health care organizations, research institutions, or publishing firms on a contract or hourly basis. They may specialize in writing about a specific scientific or medical subject for one or two clients, or they may write about a broad range of subjects for a number of different clients. Many freelance writers write articles, papers, or reports and then attempt to get them published in newspapers, trade, or consumer publications.

Requirements

High School

If you are considering a career as a writer, you should take English, journalism, and communication courses in high school. Computer classes will also be helpful. If you know in high school that you want to do scientific or medical writing, it would be to your advantage to take biology, physiology, chemistry, physics, math, health, and other science-related courses. If your school offers journalism courses and you have the chance to work on the school newspaper or yearbook, you should take advantage of this opportunity. Part-time employment at health care facilities, newspapers, publishing companies, or scientific research facilities can also provide experience and insight regarding this career. Volunteer opportunities are usually available in hospitals and nursing homes as well.

Postsecondary Training

Although not all writers are college-educated, today's jobs almost always require a bachelor's degree. Many writers earn an undergraduate degree in English, journalism, or liberal arts and then obtain a master's degree in a communications field such as medical or science writing. A good liberal arts education is important since you are often required to write about many subject areas. Science and medical-related courses are highly recommended. You should investigate internship programs that give you experience in the communications department of a corporation, medical institution, or research facility. Some newspapers, magazines, or public relations firms also have internships that give you the opportunity to write.

Some people find that after working as a writer, their interests are strong in the medical or science fields and they evolve into that writing specialty. They may return to school and enter a master's degree program or take some additional courses related specifically to science and medical writing. Similarly, science majors or people in the medical fields may find that they like the writing aspect of their jobs and return to school to pursue a career as a medical or science writer.

Certification or Licensing

Certification is not mandatory; however, certification programs are available from various organizations and institutions. The American Medical Writers Association Education Program offers an extensive continuing education and certification program.

Other Requirements

If you are considering a career as a medical or science writer, you should enjoy writing, be able to write well, and be able to express your ideas and those of others clearly. You should have an excellent knowledge of the English language and have superb grammar and spelling skills. You should be skilled in research techniques and be computer literate and familiar with software programs related to writing and publishing. You should be a curious person, enjoy learning about new things, and have an interest in science or medicine. You need to be detail-oriented since many of your writing assignments will require that you obtain and relay accurate and detailed information. Interpersonal skills are important too since many jobs require that you interact with and interview professional people such as scientists, engineers, researchers, and medical personnel. You must be able to meet deadlines and work under pressure.

Exploring

As a high school or college student, you can test your interest and aptitude in the field of writing by serving as a reporter or writer on school newspapers, yearbooks, and literary magazines. Attending writing workshops and taking writing classes will give you the opportunity to practice and sharpen your skills.

Community newspapers and local radio stations often welcome contributions from outside sources, although they may not have the resources to pay for them. Jobs in bookstores, magazine shops, libraries, and even newsstands offer a chance to become familiar with various publications. If you are interested in science writing, try to get a part-time job in a research laboratory, interview science writers, and read good science writing in major newspapers such as *The New York Times* or *The Wall Street Journal*. Similarly, if your interest is medical writing, work or volunteer in a health care facility, visit with people who do medical writing, and read medical articles in those newspapers previously listed.

Information on writing as a career may also be obtained by visiting local newspapers, publishing houses, or radio and television stations and interviewing some of the writers who work there. Career conferences and other guidance programs frequently include speakers from local or national organizations who can provide information on communication careers.

Some professional organizations such as the Society for Technical Communication welcome students as members and have special student membership rates and career information. In addition, participation in professional organizations gives you the opportunity to meet and visit with people in this career field.

Employers

Pharmaceutical and drug companies, medical research institutions, government organizations, insurance companies, health care facilities, nonprofit organizations, medical publishers, medical associations, and other medical-related industries employ medical writers.

Science writers may also be employed by medical-related industries. In addition, they are employed by scientific research companies, government research facilities, federal, state, and local agencies, manufacturing companies, research and development departments of corporations, and the chemical industries. Large universities and hospitals often employ science writers. Large technology-based corporations and industrial research groups also hire science writers.

Many science and medical writers are employed, often on a freelance basis, by newspapers, magazines, and the broadcast industries as well. Internet publishing is a growing field that hires science and medical writers. Corporations who deal with the medical or science industries also hire specialty writers as their public information officers or to head up communications departments within their facilities.

Starting Out

A fair amount of experience is required to gain a high-level position in this field. Most writers start out in entry-level positions. These jobs may be listed with college placement offices, or you may apply directly to the employment departments of corporations, institutions, universities, research facilities, nonprofit organizations, and government facilities that hire science and medical writers. Many firms now hire writers directly upon application or recommendation of college professors and placement offices. Want ads in newspapers and trade journals are another source for jobs. Serving an internship in college can give you the advantage of knowing people who can give you personal recommendations.

Internships are also excellent ways to build your portfolio. Employers in the communications field are usually interested in seeing samples of your published writing assembled in an organized portfolio or scrapbook. Working on your college's magazine or newspaper staff can help you build that portfolio. Sometimes small, regional magazines will also buy articles or assign short pieces for you to write. You should attempt to build your portfolio with good writing samples. Be sure to include the type of writing you are interested in doing, if possible.

You may need to begin your career as a junior writer or editor and work your way up. This usually involves library research, preparation of rough drafts for part or all of a report, cataloging, and other related writing tasks. These are generally carried on under the supervision of a senior writer.

Many science and medical writers enter the field after working in public relations departments, the medical profession, or science-related industries. They may use their skills to transfer to specialized writing positions or they may take additional courses or graduate work that focuses on writing or documentation skills.

Advancement

Writers with an undergraduate degree may choose to get a graduate degree in science or medical writing, corporate communications, document design, or a related program. An advanced degree may open doors to advanced careers.

Many experienced science and medical writers are often promoted to head writing, documentation, or public relations departments within corporations or institutions. Some may become recognized experts in their field and their writings may be in demand by trade journals, newspapers, magazines, and the broadcast industry.

As freelance writers prove themselves and work successfully with clients, they may be able to demand increased contract fees or hourly rates.

Earnings

Although there are no specific salary studies for science and medical writers, other writers' salary information is available.

The Society of Technical Communicators' 1999 salary survey of its members reported that the mean salary of its members was $47,560. The entry-level salary was reported to be $36,870, with the senior-level supervisor earning $58,970.

The Bureau of Labor Statistics reports that the mean annual wage for writers and editors in 1998 was $36,480. A survey of technical writers and editors conducted that same year showed that their pay was higher. The mean annual wage for technical writers and editors was $39,200.

Freelance writers' earnings can vary depending on their expertise, reputation, and the articles they are contracted to write.

Most full-time writing positions offer the usual benefits such as insurance, sick leave, and paid vacation. Some jobs also provide tuition reimbursement and retirement benefits. Freelance writers must pay for their own insurance. However, there are professional associations that may offer group insurance rates for its members.

Work Environment

Work environment depends on the type of science or medical writing and the employer. Generally, writers work in an office or research environment. Writers for the news media sometimes work in noisy surroundings. Some writers travel to research information and conduct interviews while other employers may confine research to local libraries or the Internet. In addition, some employers require writers to conduct research interviews over the phone, rather than in person.

Although the workweek usually runs 35 to 40 hours in a normal office setting, many writers may have to work overtime to cover a story, interview people, meet deadlines, or to disseminate information in a timely manner. The newspaper and broadcasting industries deliver the news 24 hours a day, seven days a week. Writers often work nights and weekends to meet press deadlines or to cover a late-developing story.

Each day may bring new and interesting situations. Some stories may even take writers to exotic locations with a chance to interview famous people and write about timely topics. Other assignments may be boring or they may take place in less than desirable settings where interview subjects may be rude and unwilling to talk. One of the most difficult elements for writers may be meeting deadlines or gathering information. People who are the most content as writers work well with deadline pressure.

Outlook

According to the Bureau of Labor Statistics, there is a lot of competition for writing and editing jobs; however, the demand for writers and editors is expected to grow faster than the average through 2008.

The Society for Technical Communication also states that there is a growing demand for technical communicators. They report that it is one of the fastest growing professions and that this growth has created a variety of career options.

As we witness advances in medicine and science, we will continue to need skilled writers to relay that information to the public and other professionals.

For More Information

The following organizations provide information on careers as science and medical writers.

American Medical Writers Association
40 West Gude Drive, Suite 101
Rockville, MD 20850-1192
Tel: 301-294-5303
Web: http://www.amwa.org

National Association of Science Writers, Inc.
PO Box 294
Greenlawn, NY 11740
Tel: 516-757-5664
Web: http://www.nasw.org

The Society for Technical Communication offers student membership for persons enrolled in a program in preparation for a career in technical communication. This organization also has a scholarship program.

Society for Technical Communication
901 North Stuart Street, Suite 904
Arlington, VA 22203-1822
Tel: 703-522-4114
Web: http://www.stac-va.org

Technical Writers and Editors

School Subjects	Business English
Personal Skills	Communication/ideas Technical/scientific
Work Environment	Primarily indoors Primarily one location
Minimum Education Level	Bachelor's degree
Salary Range	$28,600 to $44,800 to $72,000
Certification or Licensing	None available
Outlook	Faster than the average

Overview

Technical writers, sometimes called *technical communicators*, express technical and scientific ideas in easy-to-understand language. *Technical editors* revise written text to correct any errors and make it read smoothly and clearly. They also may coordinate the activities of technical writers, technical illustrators, and other staff in preparing material for publication and oversee the document development and production processes.

History

Humans have used writing as a means to communicate information for over 5,500 years. Technical writing, though, did not emerge as a specific profession in the United States until the early years of the 20th century. Before that time, engineers, scientists, and researchers did any necessary writing themselves.

During the early 1900s, technology rapidly expanded. The use of machines to manufacture and mass-produce a wide number of products paved the way for more complex and technical products. Scientists and researchers were discovering new technologies and applications for technology, particularly in electronics, medicine, and engineering. The need to record studies and research, and report them to others, grew. Also, as products became more complex, it was necessary to provide information that documented their components, showed how they were assembled, and explained how to install, use, and repair them. By the mid-1920s, writers were being used to help engineers and scientists document their work and prepare technical information for nontechnical audiences.

Editors had been used for many years to work with printers and authors. They often checked copies of a printed document to correct any errors made during printing, to rewrite unclear passages, and to correct errors in spelling, grammar, and punctuation. As the need for technical writers grew, so too did the need for technical editors. Editors became more involved in documents before the printing stage and worked closely with writers as they prepared their materials. Today, many editors coordinate the activities of all the people involved in preparing technical communications and manage the document development and production processes.

The need for technical writers grew still more with the growth of the computer industry beginning in the 1960s. Originally, many computer companies used computer programmers to write user manuals and other documentation. It was widely assumed that the material was so complex that only those who were involved with creating computer programs would be able to write about them. Although computer programmers had the technical knowledge, many were not able to write clear, easy-to-use manuals. Complaints about the difficulty using and understanding manuals were common. By the 1970s, computer companies began to hire technical writers to write computer manuals and documents. Today, this is one of the largest areas in which technical writers are employed.

The need for technical marketing writers also grew as a result of expanding computer technology. Many copywriters who worked for advertising agencies and marketing firms did not have the technical background to be able to describe the features of the technical products that were coming to market. Thus grew the need for writers who could combine the ability to promote products with the ability to communicate technical information.

The nature of technical writers' and technical editors' jobs continues to change with emerging technologies. Today, the ability to store, transmit, and receive information through computers and electronic means is changing the very nature of documents. Traditional books and paper documents are being replaced by floppy disks, CD-ROMs, interactive multimedia documents, and material accessed through bulletin board systems, faxes, the World Wide Web, and the Internet.

The Job

Technical writers and editors prepare a wide variety of documents and materials. The most common types of documents they produce are manuals, technical reports, specifications, and proposals. Some technical writers also write scripts for videos and audiovisual presentations and text for multimedia programs. Technical writers and editors prepare manuals that give instructions and detailed information on how to install, assemble, use, service, or repair a product or equipment. They may write and edit manuals as simple as a two-page leaflet that gives instructions on how to assemble a bicycle or as complex as a 500-page document that tells service technicians how to repair machinery, medical equipment, or a climate-control system. One of the most common types of manuals is the computer software manual, which informs users on how to load software on their computers, explains how to use the program, and gives information on different features.

Technical writers and editors also prepare technical reports on a multitude of subjects. These reports include documents that give the results of research and laboratory tests and documents that describe the progress of a project. They also write and edit sales proposals, product specifications, quality standards, journal articles, in-house style manuals, and newsletters.

The work of a technical writer begins when he or she is assigned to prepare a document. The writer meets with members of an account or technical team to learn the requirements for the document, the intended purpose or objectives, and the audience. During the planning stage, the writer learns when the document needs to be completed, approximately how long it should be, whether artwork or illustrations are to be included, who the other team members are, and any other production or printing requirements. A schedule is created that defines the different stages of development and determines when the writer needs to have certain parts of the document ready.

The next step in document development is the research, or information gathering, phase. During this stage, technical writers gather all the available information about the product or subject, read and review it, and determine what other information is needed. They may research the topic by reading technical publications, but in most cases they will need to gather information directly from the people working on the product. Writers meet with and interview people who are sources of information, such as scientists, engineers, software developers, computer programmers, managers, and project managers. They ask questions, listen, and take notes or tape record interviews. They gather any available notes, drawings, or diagrams that may be useful.

After writers gather all the necessary information, they sort it out and organize it. They plan how they are going to present the information and prepare an outline for the document. They may decide how the document will look and prepare the design, format, and layout of the pages. In some cases, this may be done by an editor rather than the writer. If illustrations, diagrams, or photographs are going to be included, either the editor or writer makes arrangements for an illustrator, photographer, or art researcher to produce or obtain them.

Then, the writer starts writing and prepares a rough draft of the document. If the document is very large, a writer may prepare it in segments. Once the rough draft is completed, it is submitted to a designated person or group for technical review. Copies of the draft are distributed to managers, engineers, or subject matter experts who can easily determine if any technical information is inaccurate or missing. These reviewers read the document and suggest changes.

The rough draft is also given to technical editors for review of a variety of factors. The editors check that the material is organized well, that each section flows with the section before and after it, and that the language is appropriate for the intended audience. They also check for correct use of grammar, spelling, and punctuation. They ensure that names of parts or objects are consistent throughout the document and that references are accurate. They also check the labeling of graphs and captions for accuracy. Technical editors use special symbols, called proofreader's marks, to indicate the types of changes needed.

The editor and reviewers return their copies of the document to the technical writer. The writer incorporates the appropriate suggestions and revisions and prepares the final draft. The final draft is once again submitted to a designated reviewer or team of reviewers. In some cases, the technical reviewer may do a quick check to make sure that the requested changes were made. In other cases, the technical reviewer may examine the document in depth to ensure technical accuracy and correctness. A walkthrough, or test of the document, may be done for certain types of documents. For example, a walkthrough may be done for a document that explains how to assemble a product. A tester assembles the product by following the instructions given in the document. The tester makes a note of all sections that are unclear or inaccurate, and the document is returned to the writer for any necessary revisions.

For some types of documents, a legal review may also be done. For example, a pharmaceutical company that is preparing a training manual to teach its sales representatives about a newly released drug needs to ensure that all materials are in compliance with Food and Drug Administration (FDA) requirements. A member of the legal department who is familiar with these requirements will review the document to make sure that all information in the document conforms to FDA rules.

Once the final draft has been approved, the document is submitted to the technical editor who makes a comprehensive and detailed check of the document. In addition to checking that the language is clear and reads smoothly, the editor makes sure the table of contents matches the different sections or chapters of a document, all illustrations and diagrams are correctly placed, all captions are matched to the correct picture, consistent terminology is used, and correct references are used in the bibliography and text.

The editor returns the document to either the writer or a word processor who makes any necessary corrections. This copy is then checked by a *proofreader*. The proofreader compares the final copy against the editor's marked-up copy and makes sure that all changes were made. The document is then prepared for printing. In some cases, the writer is responsible for preparing camera-ready copy or electronic files for printing purposes, and in other cases, a print production coordinator prepares all material to submit to a printer.

Some technical writers specialize in a specific type of material. *Technical marketing writers* create promotional and marketing materials for technological products. They may write the copy for an advertisement for a technical product, such as a computer workstation or software, or write press releases about the product. They also write sales literature, product flyers, Web pages, and multimedia presentations.

Other technical writers prepare scripts for videotapes and films about technical subjects. These writers, called *scriptwriters*, need to have an understanding of film and video production techniques.

Some technical writers and editors prepare articles for scientific, medical, computer, or engineering trade journals. These articles may report the results of research conducted by doctors, scientists, or engineers or report on technological advances in a particular field. Some technical writers and editors also develop textbooks.They may receive articles written by engineers or scientists and edit and revise them to make them more suitable for the intended audience.

Technical writers and editors may create documents for a variety of media. Electronic media, such as compact discs and online services, are increasingly being used in place of books and paper documents. Technical writers may create materials that are accessed through bulletin board systems and the Internet or create computer-based resources, such as help menus on computer programs. They also create interactive, multimedia documents that are distributed on compact discs or floppy disks. Some of these media require knowledge of special computer programs that allow material to be hyperlinked, or electronically cross-referenced.

Requirements

High School

In high school, you should take composition, grammar, literature, creative writing, journalism, social studies, math, statistics, engineering, computer science, and as many science classes as possible. Business courses are also useful as they explain the organizational structure of companies and how they operate.

Postsecondary Training

Most employers prefer to hire technical writers and editors who have bachelor's or advanced degrees. Many technical editors graduate with degrees in the humanities, especially English or journalism. Technical writers typically need to have a strong foundation in engineering, computers, or science. Many technical writers graduate with degrees in engineering or science and take classes in technical writing.

Many different types of college programs are available that prepare people to become technical writers and editors. A growing number of colleges are offering degrees in technical writing. Schools without a technical writing program may offer degrees in journalism or English. Programs are offered through English, communications, and journalism departments. Classes vary based on the type of program. In general, classes for technical writers include a core curriculum in writing and classes in algebra, statistics, logic, science, engineering, and computer programming languages. Useful classes for editors include technical writing, project management, grammar, proofreading, copyediting, and print production.

Many technical writers and editors earn master's degrees. In these programs, they study technical writing in depth and may specialize in a certain area, such as scriptwriting, instructional design, or multimedia applications. In addition, many nondegree writing programs are offered to technical writers and editors to hone their skills. Offered as extension courses or continuing education courses, these programs include courses on indexing, editing medical materials, writing for trade journals, and other related subjects.

Technical writers, and occasionally technical editors, are often asked to present samples of their work. College students should build a portfolio during their college years in which they collect their best samples from work that they may have done for a literary magazine, newsletter, or yearbook.

Technical writers and editors should be willing to pursue learning throughout their careers. As technology changes, technical writers and editors may need to take classes to update their knowledge. Changes in electronic printing and computer technology will also change the way technical writers and editors do their jobs and they may need to take courses to learn new skills or new technologies.

Other Requirements

Technical writers need to have good communications skills, science and technical aptitudes, and the ability to think analytically. Technical editors also need to have good communications skills, and judgment, as well as the ability to identify and correct errors in written material. They need to be diplomatic, assertive, and able to explain tactfully what needs to be corrected to writers, engineers, and other people involved with a document. Technical editors should be able to understand technical information easily, but they need less scientific and technical backgrounds than writers. Both technical writers and editors need to be able to work as part of a team and collaborate with others on a project. They need to be highly self-motivated, well organized, and able to work under pressure.

Exploring

If you enjoy writing and are considering a career in technical writing or editing, you should make writing a daily activity. Writing is a skill that develops over time and through practice. Students can keep journals, join writing clubs, and practice different types of writing, such as scriptwriting and informative reports. Sharing writing with others and asking them to critique it is especially helpful. Comments from readers on what they enjoyed about a piece of writing or difficulty they had in understanding certain sections provides valuable feedback that helps to improve your writing style.

Reading a variety of materials is also helpful. Reading exposes you to both good and bad writing styles and techniques and helps you to identify why one approach works better than another.

You may also gain experience by working on a literary magazine, student newspaper, or yearbook (or starting one of your own if one is not available). Both writing and editing articles and managing production give you the opportunity to learn new skills and to see what is involved in preparing documents and other materials.

Students may also be able to get internships, cooperative education assignments, or summer or part-time jobs as proofreaders or editorial assistants that may include writing responsibilities.

Employers

Employment may be found in many different types of places, such as in the fields of aerospace, computers, engineering, pharmacy, and research and development, or with the nuclear industry, medical publishers, government agencies or contractors, and colleges and universities. The aerospace, engineering, medical, and computer industries hire significant numbers of technical writers and editors. So does the federal government, particularly in the departments of Defense and Agriculture, the National Aeronautics and Space Administration (NASA), and the Atomic Energy Commission.

Starting Out

Many technical writers start their careers as scientists, engineers, technicians, or research assistants and move into writing after several years of experience in those positions. Technical writers with a bachelor's degree in a technical subject such as engineering may be able to find work as a technical writer immediately upon graduating from college, but many employers prefer to hire writers with some work experience.

Technical editors who graduate with a bachelor's degree in English or journalism may find entry-level work as editorial assistants, copy editors, or proofreaders. From these positions they are able to move into technical editing positions. Or beginning workers may find jobs as technical editors in small companies or those with a small technical communications department.

If you plan to work for the federal government, you need to pass an examination. Information about examinations and job openings is available at federal employment centers.

You may learn about job openings through your college's job placement services and want ads in newspapers and professional magazines. You may also research companies that hire technical writers and editors and apply directly to them. Many libraries provide useful job resource guides and directories that provide information about companies that hire in specific areas.

Advancement

As technical writers and editors gain experience, they move into more challenging and responsible positions. At first, they may work on simple documents or be assigned to work on sections of a document. As they demonstrate their proficiency and skills, they are given more complex assignments and are responsible for more activities.

Technical writers and editors with several years of experience may move into project management positions. As project managers, they are responsible for the entire document development and production processes. They schedule and budget resources and assign writers, editors, illustrators, and other workers to a project. They monitor the schedule, supervise workers, and ensure that costs remain in budget.

Technical writers and editors who show good project management skills, leadership abilities, and good interpersonal skills may become supervisors or managers. Both technical writers and editors can move into senior writer and senior editor positions. These positions involve increased responsibilities and may include supervising other workers.

Many technical writers and editors seek to develop and perfect their skills rather than move into management or supervisory positions. As they gain a reputation for their quality of work, they may be able to select choice assignments. They may learn new skills as a means of being able to work in new areas. For example, a technical writer may learn a new desktop program in order to become more proficient in designing. Or, a technical writer may learn a hypermedia or hypertext computer program in order to be able to create a multimedia program. Technical writers and editors who broaden their skill base and capabilities can move to higher-paying positions within their own company or at another company. They also may work as freelancers or set up their own communications companies.

Earnings

In the late 1990s, the average salary for technical writers and editors was $48,000. Salaries for entry-level technical writers and editors ranged from slightly less than $28,600 to more than $44,800. Writers and editors with more than 10 years of experience earned annual salaries between $45,000 and $67,000. Senior writers and editors with management responsibilities earned salaries as high as $72,000 a year. The average annual salary for technical writers and editors in the federal government was $47,440 in 1996. Writers and editors in the computer industry earn slightly higher average salaries than in other industries, about $39,200 in 1997. In general, writers and editors who work for firms with large writing staffs earn more than those who work at companies with less than ten writers and editors.

Most companies offer benefits that include paid holidays and vacations, medical insurance, and 401(k) plans. They may also offer profit sharing, pension plans, and tuition assistance programs.

Work Environment

Technical writers and editors usually work in an office environment, with well-lighted and quiet surroundings. They may have their own offices or share work space with other writers and editors. Most writers and editors have computers. They may be able to utilize the services of support staff who can word process revisions, run off copies, fax material, and perform other administrative functions or they may have to perform all of these tasks themselves.

Some technical writers and editors work out of home offices and use computer modems and networks to send and receive materials electronically. They may go in to the office only on occasion for meetings and gathering information. Freelancers and contract workers may work at a company's premises or at home.

Although the standard workweek is 40 hours, many technical writers and editors frequently work 50 or 60 hours a week. Job interruptions, meetings, and conferences can prevent writers from having long periods of time to write. Therefore, many writers work after hours or bring work home. Both writers and editors frequently work in the evening or on weekends in order to meet a deadline.

In many companies there is pressure to produce documents as quickly as possible. Both technical writers and editors may feel at times that they are compromising the quality of their work due to the need to conform to time and budget constraints. In some companies, technical writers and editors may have increased workloads due to company reorganizations or downsizing. They may need to do the work that was formerly done by more than one person. Technical writers and editors also are increasingly assuming roles and responsibilities formerly performed by other people and this can increase work pressures and stress.

Despite these pressures, most technical writers and editors gain immense satisfaction from their work and the roles that they perform in producing technical communications.

Outlook

The writing and editing field is generally very competitive. Each year, there are more people trying to enter this field than there are available openings. The field of technical writing and editing, though, offers more opportunities than other areas of writing and editing, such as book publishing or journalism. Employment opportunities for technical writers and editors are expected to grow faster than average through 2008. Demand is growing for technical writers who can produce well-written computer manuals. In addition to the computer industry, the pharmaceutical industry is showing an increased need for technical writers. Currently, around 50,000 people are employed as technical writers and editors.

Writers may find positions that include duties in addition to writing. A growing trend is for companies to use writers to run a department, supervise other writers, and manage freelance writers and outside contractors. In addition, many writers are acquiring responsibilities that include desktop publishing and print production coordination.

The demand for technical writers and editors is significantly affected by the economy. During recessionary times, technical writers and editors are often among the first to be let go. Many companies today are continuing to downsize or reduce their number of employees and are reluctant to keep writers on staff. Such companies prefer to hire writers and editors on a temporary contract basis, using them only as long as it takes to complete an assigned document. Technical writers and editors who work on a temporary or freelance basis need to market their services and continually look for new assignments. They also do not have the security or benefits offered by full-time employment.

For More Information

For information on careers, please contact:

Society for Technical Communication
901 North Stuart Street, Suite 904
Arlington, VA 22203-1822
Tel: 703-522-4114
Email: stc@stc-va.org
Web: http://www.stc-va.org

Webmasters

Computer science Mathematics	School Subjects
Communication/ideas Technical/scientific	Personal Skills
Primarily indoors Primarily one location	Work Environment
Some postsecondary training	Minimum Education Level
$25,000 to $35,000 to $100,000	Salary Range
Voluntary	Certification or Licensing
Much faster than the average	Outlook

Overview

Webmasters design, implement, and maintain World Wide Web sites for corporations, educational institutions, not-for-profit organizations, government agencies, or other institutions. Webmasters should have working knowledge of network configurations, interface, graphic design, software development, business, writing, marketing, and project management. Because the function of a webmaster encompasses so many different responsibilities, the position is often held by a team of individuals, rather than a single person, in a large organization.

The Job

Because the idea of designing and maintaining a Web site is relatively new, there is no complete, definitive job description for a webmaster. Many of their job responsibilities depend upon the goals and needs of the particular organization for which they work. There are, however, some basic duties that are common to almost all webmasters.

The webmaster, specifically site managers, first secures space on the Web for the site he or she is developing. This is done by contracting with an Internet service provider. The provider serves as a sort of storage facility for the organization's on-line information, usually charging a set monthly fee for a specified amount of megabyte space. The webmaster may also be responsible for establishing a URL (Uniform Resource Locator) for the Web site he or she is developing. The URL serves as the site's on-line "address," and must be registered with InterNIC, the Web URL registration service.

The webmaster is responsible for developing the actual Web site for his or her organization. In some cases, this may involve actually writing the text content of the pages. More commonly, however, the webmaster is given the text to be used, and is merely responsible for programming it in such a way that it can be displayed on a Web page. In larger companies webmasters specialize in content, adaptation, and presentation of data.

In order for text to be displayed on a Web page, it must be formatted using HyperText Markup Language (HTML). HTML is a system of coding text so that the computer that is "reading" it knows how to display it. For example, text could be coded to be a certain size or color or to be italicized or boldface. Paragraphs, line breaks, alignment, and margins are other examples of text attributes that must be coded in HTML.

Although it is less and less common, some webmasters code text manually, by actually typing the various commands into the body of the text. This method is time-consuming, however, and mistakes are easily made. More often, webmasters use a software program that automatically codes text. Some word processing programs, such as WordPerfect, even offer HTML options.

Along with coding the text, the webmaster must lay out the elements of the Web site in such a way that it is visually pleasing, well organized, and easy to navigate. He or she may use various colors, background patterns, images, tables, or charts. These graphic elements can come from image files already on the Web, software clip art files, or images scanned into the computer with an electronic scanner. In some cases, when an organization is using the Web site to promote its product or service, the webmaster may work with a marketing specialist or department to develop a page.

Some Web sites have several directories or "layers." That is, an organization may have several Web pages, organized in a sort of "tree," with its home page connected, via hypertext links, to other pages, which may in turn be linked to other pages. The webmaster is responsible for organizing the pages in such a way that a visitor can easily browse through them and find what he or she is looking for. Such webmasters are called *programmers* and *developers*; they are also responsible for creating Web tools and special Web functionality.

For webmasters who work for organizations that have several different Web sites, one responsibility may be making sure that the "style" or appearance of all the pages is the same. This is often referred to as "house style." In large organizations, such as universities, where many different departments may be developing and maintaining their own pages, it is especially important that the webmaster monitor these pages to ensure consistency and conformity to the organization's requirements. In almost every case, the webmaster has the final authority for the content and appearance of his or her organization's Web site. He or she must carefully edit, proofread, and check the appearance of every page.

Besides designing and setting up Web sites, most webmasters are charged with maintaining and updating existing sites. Most sites contain information that changes regularly. Some change daily, or even hourly. Depending upon his or her employer and the type of Web site, the webmaster may spend a good deal of time updating and remodeling the page. He or she is also responsible for ensuring that the hyperlinks contained within the Web site lead to the sites they should. Since it is common for links to change or become obsolete, the webmaster usually performs a link check every few weeks.

Other job duties vary, depending upon the employer and the position. Most webmasters are responsible for receiving and answering email messages from visitors to the organization's Web site. Some webmasters keep logs and create reports on when and how often their pages are visited and by whom. Depending on the company, Web sites count anywhere from 300 to 1.4 billion visits, or "hits," a month. Some create and maintain order forms or on-line "shopping carts" that allow visitors to the Web site to purchase products or services. Some may train other employees on how to create or update Web pages. Finally, webmasters may be responsible for developing and adhering to a budget for their departments.

Requirements

High School

High school students who are interested in becoming a webmaster should take as many computer science classes as they can. Mathematics classes are also helpful. Finally, because writing skills are important in this career, English classes are good choices.

Postsecondary Training

As of today, there is no set advanced educational path or requirement for becoming a webmaster. While many have bachelor's degrees in computer science, liberal arts degrees, such as English, are not uncommon. There are also webmasters who have degrees in engineering, mathematics, and marketing. Not all webmasters have bachelor's degrees, however; some have two-year degrees, or a high school education only. Currently, most webmasters do not have formal, specific training in how to design Web sites.

Certification or Licensing

There is strong debate within the industry regarding certification. Some, mostly corporate CEOs, favor certification. They view certification as a way to gauge an employee's skill and Web mastery expertise. Others argue, however, that is nearly impossible to test knowledge of technology that is constantly changing and improving. Despite the split of opinion, webmaster certification programs are available at many colleges, universities, and technical schools throughout the United States. Programs vary in length, anywhere from three weeks, to nine months or more; topics covered include client/server technology, Web development, programs, and software and hardware. The International Webmasters Association also offers a voluntary certification program.

Should webmasters be certified? Though it's currently not a prerequisite for employment, certification can only enhance a candidate's chance at landing a webmaster position.

What most webmasters have in common is a strong knowledge of computer technology. Most people who enter this field are already well-versed in computer operating systems, programming languages, computer graphics, and Internet standards. When considering candidates for the position of webmaster, employers usually require at least two years of experience with World Wide Web technologies. In some cases, employers require that candidates already have experience in designing and maintaining Web sites. It is, in fact, most common for someone to move into the position of webmaster from another computer-related job in the same organization.

Other Requirements

Webmasters should be creative. It is important for a Web page to be well designed in order to attract attention. Good writing skills and an aptitude for marketing are also excellent qualities for anyone considering a career in Web site design.

Exploring

One of the easiest ways to learn about what a webmaster does is to spend time "surfing" on the World Wide Web. By examining a variety of Web sites to see how they look and operate, you can begin to get a feel for what goes into a home page.

An even better way to explore this career is to design your own personal Web page. Many Internet servers offer their users the option of designing and maintaining a personal Web page for a very low fee. A personal page can contain virtually anything that you want to include, from snapshots of friends to audio files of favorite music to hypertext links to other favorite sites.

Employers

Webmasters are employed by Web design companies, businesses, schools or universities, not-for-profit organizations, government agencies—in short, any organization that requires a presence on the World Wide Web. Webmasters may also work as freelancers or operate their own Web design business.

Starting Out

Most people become webmasters by moving into the position from another computer-related position within the same company. Since most large organizations already use computers for various functions, they may employ a person or several people to serve as computer "specialists." If these organizations decide to develop their own Web sites, they frequently assign the task to one of these employees who is already experienced with the computer system. Often, the person who ultimately becomes an organization's webmaster at first just takes on the job in addition to his or her other, already-established duties.

Another way that individuals find jobs in this field is through on-line postings of job openings. Many companies post webmaster position openings on-line because the candidates they hope to attract are very likely to use the Internet for a job search. Therefore, the prospective webmaster should use the World Wide Web to check job-related newsgroups. He or she might also use a Web search engine to locate openings.

Advancement

Experienced webmasters employed by a large organization may be able to advance to a supervisory position in which he or she directs the work of a team of webmasters. Others might advance by starting their own business, designing Web sites on a contract basis for several clients, rather than working exclusively for one organization.

Opportunities for webmasters of the future are endless due to the continuing development of on-line technology. As understanding and use of the World Wide Web increase, there may be new or expanded job duties for individuals with expertise in this field. People working today as webmasters may be required in a few years to perform jobs that don't even exist yet.

Earnings

According to *U.S. News & World Report,* salaries for the position of webmaster range from $50,000 to $100,000 per year. The demand for webmasters is so great that some companies are offering stock options, sign-on bonuses, and other perks, in addition to salaries from $80,000 to $110,000. While this may be true for those who are hired into an organization specifically to fill the position, it is not representative of the many webmasters who have merely moved into the position from another position within their company or have taken on the task in addition to other duties. These employees are often paid approximately the same salary they were already making. According to the 1998 Webmaster Survey, the majority of webmasters earn under $50,000. Nineteen percent of all webmasters earned from $25,000 to $40,999 annually; 17 percent earned less than $25,000.

Depending upon the organization for which they work, webmasters may receive a benefits package in addition to salary. A typical benefits package would include paid vacations and holidays, medical insurance, and perhaps a pension plan.

Work Environment

Although much of the webmaster's day may be spent alone, it is nonetheless important that he or she be able to communicate and work well with others. Depending upon the organization for which he or she works, the webmaster may have periodic meetings with graphic designers, marketing specialists, writers, or other professionals who have input into the Web site development. In many larger organizations, there is a team of webmasters, rather than just one. Although each team member works alone on his or her own specific duties, the members may meet frequently to discuss and coordinate their activities.

Because technology changes so rapidly, this job is constantly evolving. Webmasters must spend time reading and learning about new developments in on-line communication. They may be continually working with new computer software or hardware. Their actual job responsibilities may even change, as the capabilities of both the organization and the World Wide Web itself expand. It is important that these employees be flexible and willing to learn and grow with the technology that drives their work.

Because they don't deal with the general public, most webmasters are allowed to wear fairly casual attire and to work in a relaxed atmosphere. In most cases, the job calls for standard working hours, although there may be times when overtime is required.

Outlook

There can be no doubt that computer—and specifically on-line—technology will continue its rapid growth for the next several years. Likewise, then, the number of computer-related jobs, including that of webmaster, should also increase. The World Organization of Webmasters projects an explosion of jobs available through 2008—well over 8 million. The majority of webmasters working today are full-time employees—about 86 percent according to the 1998 Webmaster Study, conducted by Collaborative Marketing. The newness of this job is reflected in the age demographics of webmasters—35 percent are between the ages of 26 and 35 (1998 Webmaster Study); and according to *Web Week*, 72 percent are in their first webmaster position. This indicates the attraction of the young to the Internet, and to better tap that market, a company's desire to fill webmaster positions with young comput-er-savvy individuals.

The 1998 Webmaster Study found this field to be currently male-domi-nated. However, there is great opportunity for women in this field. Many large companies, such as Wal-Mart, are looking for talented individuals who, according to a Wal-Mart webmaster (yes, female) "can combine a lot of tech-nical knowledge with the ability to cooperate with people who don't know a lot of technology. Women can often be very good at that."

As more and more businesses, not-for-profit organizations, educational institutions, and government agencies choose to "go online," the total num-ber of Web sites will grow, as will the need for experts to design them. Companies are starting to view Web sites as more than a temporary experi-ment, but rather an important and necessary business and marketing tool. Growth will be largest with Internet content developers—webmasters responsible for the information displayed on a Web site. The 1998 Webmaster Study predicts Internet content developers will become more sophisticated with their techniques and will significantly surpass the growth of the technical segment of webmasters.

One thing to keep in mind, however, is that when technology advances extremely rapidly, it tends to make old methods of doing things obsolete. If current trends continue, the role and role of webmaster will be carried out by a group or department instead of a single employee, in order to keep up with the demands of the position. It is possible that in the next few years, changes in technology will make the Web sites we are now familiar with a thing of the past. Another possibility is that, like desktop publishing, user-friendly software programs will make Web site design so easy and efficient that it no longer requires an "expert" to do it well. Webmasters who are con-cerned with job security should be willing to continue learning and using the very latest developments in technology, so that they are prepared to move into the future of online communication, whatever it may be.

For More Information

The Association of Internet Professionals represents the worldwide community of people employed in Internet-related fields.

Association of Internet Professionals
15 East 26th Street, Suite 1403
New York, NY 10010
Tel: 877-AIP-0800
Email: info@association.org
Web: http://www.association.org/

Visit the IWA Web site for information on educational institutions that offer web-master training, webmaster specialties, and its voluntary certification program:

International Webmasters Association (IWA)
119 East Union Street, Suite #E
Pasadena, CA 91103
Tel: 626-449-3709
Web: http://www.iwanet.org

For information on education and certification, contact:

World Organization of Webmasters
9580 Oak Avenue Parkway, Suite 7-177
Folsom, CA 95630
Tel: 916-608-1597
Email: info@joinwow.org
Web: http://www.world-webmasters.org

Writers

English Journalism	School Subjects
Communication/ideas Helping/teaching	Personal Skills
Primarily indoors Primarily one location	Work Environment
Bachelor's degree	Minimum Education Level
$20,920 to $36,480 to $76,660+	Salary Range
None available	Certification or Licensing
Faster than the average	Outlook

Overview

Writers are involved with expressing, editing, promoting, and interpreting ideas and facts in written form for books, magazines, trade journals, newspapers, technical studies and reports, company newsletters, radio and television broadcasts, and advertisements.

Writers develop fiction and nonfiction ideas for plays, novels, poems, and other related works; report, analyze, and interpret facts, events, and personalities; review art, music, drama, and other artistic presentations; and persuade the general public to choose or favor certain goods, services, and personalities.

History

The skill of writing has existed for thousands of years. Papyrus fragments with writing by ancient Egyptians date from about 3000 BC, and archaeological findings show that the Chinese had developed books by about 1300 BC. A number of technical obstacles had to be overcome before printing and the profession of writing evolved. Books of the Middle Ages were copied by hand on parchment. The ornate style that marked these books helped ensure their rarity. Also, few people were able to read. Religious fervor prohibited the reproduction of secular literature.

The development of the printing press by Johannes Gutenberg in the middle of the 15th century and the liberalism of the Protestant Reformation, which helped encourage a wider range of publications, greater literacy, and the creation of a number of works of literary merit, helped develop the publishing industry. The first authors worked directly with printers.

The modern publishing age began in the 18th century. Printing became mechanized, and the novel, magazine, and newspaper developed. The first newspaper in the American colonies appeared in the early 18th century, but it was Benjamin Franklin who, as editor and writer, made the *Pennsylvania Gazette* one of the most influential in setting a high standard for his fellow American journalists. Franklin also published the first magazine in the colonies, *The American Magazine*, in 1741.

Advances in the printing trades, photoengraving, retailing, and the availability of capital produced a boom in newspapers and magazines in the 19th century. Further mechanization in the printing field, such as the use of the Linotype machine, high-speed rotary presses, and special color reproduction processes, set the stage for still further growth in the book, newspaper, and magazine industry.

In addition to the print media, the broadcasting industry has contributed to the development of the professional writer. Film, radio, and television are sources of entertainment, information, and education that provide employment for thousands of writers.

The Job

Writers work in the field of communications. Specifically, they deal with the written word, whether it is destined for the printed page, broadcast, computer screen, or live theater. The nature of their work is as varied as the materials they produce: books, magazines, trade journals, newspapers, technical reports, company newsletters and other publications, advertisements, speeches, scripts for motion picture and stage productions, and scripts for radio and television broadcast. Writers develop ideas and write for all media.

Prose writers for newspapers, magazines, and books share many of the same duties. First they come up with an idea for an article or book from their own interests or are assigned a topic by an editor. The topic is of relevance to the particular publication; for example, a writer for a magazine on parenting may be assigned an article on car seat safety. Then writers begin gathering as much information as possible about the subject through library research, interviews, the Internet, observation, and other methods. They keep extensive notes from which they will draw material for their project. Once the material has been organized and arranged in logical sequence, writers prepare a written outline. The process of developing a piece of writing is exciting, although it can also involve detailed and solitary work. After researching an idea, a writer might discover that a different perspective or related topic would be more effective, entertaining, or marketable.

When working on assignment, writers submit their outlines to an editor or other company representative for approval. Then they write a first draft of the manuscript, trying to put the material into words that will have the desired effect on their audience. They often rewrite or polish sections of the material as they proceed, always searching for just the right way of imparting information or expressing an idea or opinion. A manuscript may be reviewed, corrected, and revised numerous times before a final copy is submitted. Even after that, an editor may request additional changes.

Writers for newspapers, magazines, or books often specialize in their subject matter. Some writers might have an educational background that allows them to give critical interpretations or analyses. For example, a health or science writer for a newspaper typically has a degree in biology and can interpret new ideas in the field for the average reader.

Columnists or *commentators* analyze news and social issues. They write about events from the standpoint of their own experience or opinion. *Critics* review literary, musical, or artistic works and performances. *Editorial writers* write on topics of public interest, and their comments, consistent with the viewpoints and policies of their employers, are intended to stimulate or mold public opinion. *Newswriters* work for newspapers, radio, or TV news departments, writing news stories from notes supplied by reporters or wire services.

Corporate writers and writers for nonprofit organizations have a wide variety of responsibilities. These writers may work in such places as a large insurance corporation or for a small nonprofit religious group where they may be required to write news releases, annual reports, speeches for the company head, or public relations materials. Typically they are assigned a topic with length requirements for a given project. They may receive raw research materials, such as statistics, and are expected to conduct additional research, including personal interviews. These writers must be able to write quickly and accurately on short deadlines, while also working with people whose primary job is not in the communications field. The written work is submitted to a supervisor and often a legal department for approval; rewrites are a normal part of this job.

Copywriters write copy that is primarily designed to sell goods and services. Their work appears as advertisements in newspapers, magazines, and other publications or as commercials on radio and television broadcasts.

Sales and marketing representatives first provide information on the product and help determine the style and length of the copy. The copywriters conduct additional research and interviews; to formulate an effective approach, they study advertising trends and review surveys of consumer preferences. Armed with this information, copywriters write a draft that is submitted to the account executive and the client for approval. The copy is often returned for correction and revision until everyone involved is satisfied. Copywriters, like corporate writers, may also write articles, bulletins, news releases, sales letters, speeches, and other related informative and promotional material. Many copywriters are employed in advertising agencies. They also may work for public relations firms or in communications departments of large companies.

Technical writers can be divided into two main groups: those who convert technical information into material for the general public, and those who convey technical information between professionals. Technical writers in the first group may prepare service manuals or handbooks, instruction or repair booklets, or sales literature or brochures; those in the second group may write grant proposals, research reports, contract specifications, or research abstracts.

Screenwriters prepare scripts for motion pictures or television. They select or are assigned a subject, conduct research, write and submit a plot outline and narrative synopsis (treatment), and confer with the producer and/or director about possible revisions. Screenwriters may adapt books or plays for film and television dramatizations. They often collaborate with other screenwriters and may specialize in a particular type of script or writing.

Playwrights do similar writing for the stage. They write dialogue and describe action for plays that may be tragedies, comedies, or dramas, with themes sometimes adapted from fictional, historical, or narrative sources. Playwrights combine the elements of action, conflict, purpose, and resolution to depict events from real or imaginary life. They often make revisions even while the play is in rehearsal.

Continuity writers prepare the material read by radio and television announcers to introduce or connect various parts of their programs.

Novelists and *short story writers* create stories that may be published in books, magazines, or literary journals. They take incidents from their own lives, from news events, or from their imaginations and create characters, settings, actions, and resolutions. *Poets* create narrative, dramatic, or lyric poetry for books, magazines, or other publications, as well as for special events such as commemorations. These writers may work with literary agents or editors who help guide them through the writing process, which includes research of the subject matter and an understanding of the intended audience. Many universities and colleges offer graduate degrees in creative writing. In these programs, students work intensively with published writers to learn the art of storytelling.

Writers can be employed either as in-house staff or as freelancers. Pay varies according to experience and the position, but freelancers must provide their own office space and equipment such as computers and fax machines. Freelancers also are responsible for keeping tax records, sending out invoices, negotiating contracts, and providing their own health insurance.

Requirements

High School

High school courses that are helpful include English, literature, foreign languages, general science, social studies, computer science, and typing. The ability to type is almost a requisite for all positions in the communications field as is familiarity with computers.

Postsecondary Training

Competition for writing jobs almost always demands the background of a college education. Many employers prefer you have a broad liberal arts background or majors in English, literature, history, philosophy, or one of the social sciences. Other employers desire communications or journalism training in college. Occasionally a master's degree in a specialized writing field may be required. A number of schools offer courses in journalism, and some of them offer courses or majors in book publishing, publication management, and newspaper and magazine writing.

In addition to formal course work, most employers look for practical writing experience. If you have served on high school or college newspapers, yearbooks, or literary magazines, you will make a better candidate, as well as if you have worked for small community newspapers or radio stations, even in an unpaid position. Many book publishers, magazines, newspapers, and radio and television stations have summer internship programs that provide valuable training if you want to learn about the publishing and broadcasting businesses. Interns do many simple tasks, such as running errands and answering phones, but some may be asked to perform research, conduct interviews, or even write some minor pieces.

Writers who specialize in technical fields may need degrees, concentrated course work, or experience in specific subject areas. This applies frequently to engineering, business, or one of the sciences. Also, technical communications is a degree now offered at many universities and colleges.

If you wish to enter positions with the federal government, you will have to take a civil service examination and meet certain specified requirements, according to the type and level of position.

Other Requirements

Writers should be creative and able to express ideas clearly, have a broad general knowledge, be skilled in research techniques, and be computer literate. Other assets include curiosity, persistence, initiative, resourcefulness, and an accurate memory. For some jobs—on a newspaper, for example, where the activity is hectic and deadlines short—the ability to concentrate and produce under pressure is essential.

Exploring

As a high school or college student, you can test your interest and aptitude in the field of writing by serving as a reporter or writer on school newspapers, yearbooks, and literary magazines. Various writing courses and workshops offer the opportunity to sharpen writing skills.

Small community newspapers and local radio stations often welcome contributions from outside sources, although they may not have the resources to pay for them. Jobs in bookstores, magazine shops, and even newsstands offer a chance to become familiar with the various publications.

Information on writing as a career may also be obtained by visiting local newspapers, publishers, or radio and television stations and interviewing some of the writers who work there. Career conferences and other guidance programs frequently include speakers on the entire field of communications from local or national organizations.

Employers

Nearly a third of salaried writers and editors work for newspapers, magazines, and book publishers, according to the *Occupational Outlook Handbook*. Writers are also employed by advertising agencies, in radio and television broadcasting, public relations firms, and on journals and newsletters published by business and nonprofit organizations, such as professional associations, labor unions, and religious organizations. Other employers are government agencies and film production companies.

Starting Out

A fair amount of experience is required to gain a high-level position in the field. Most writers start out in entry-level positions. These jobs may be listed with college placement offices, or they may be obtained by applying directly to the employment departments of the individual publishers or broadcasting companies. Graduates who previously served internships with these companies often have the advantage of knowing someone who can give them a personal recommendation. Want ads in newspapers and trade journals are another source for jobs. Because of the competition for positions, however, few vacancies are listed with public or private employment agencies.

Employers in the communications field usually are interested in samples of published writing. These are often assembled in an organized portfolio or scrapbook. Bylined or signed articles are more impressive than stories whose source is not identified.

Beginning positions as a junior writer usually involve library research, preparation of rough drafts for part or all of a report, cataloging, and other related writing tasks. These are generally carried on under the supervision of a senior writer.

Some technical writers have entered the field after working in public relations departments or as technicians or research assistants, then transferring to technical writing as openings occur. Many firms now hire writers directly upon application or recommendation of college professors and placement offices.

Advancement

Most writers find their first jobs as editorial or production assistants. Advancement may be more rapid in small companies, where beginners learn by doing a little bit of everything and may be given writing tasks immediately. In large firms, duties are usually more compartmentalized. Assistants in entry-level positions are assigned such tasks as research, fact checking, and copyrighting, but it generally takes much longer to advance to full-scale writing duties.

Promotion into more responsible positions may come with the assignment of more important articles and stories to write, or it may be the result of moving to another company. Mobility among employees in this field is common. An assistant in one publishing house may switch to an executive position in another. Or a writer may switch to a related field as a type of advancement: from publishing, for example, to teaching, public relations, advertising, radio, or television.

A technical writer can be promoted to positions of responsibility by moving from such jobs as writer to technical editor to project leader or documentation manager. Opportunities in specialized positions also are possible.

Freelance or self-employed writers earn advancement in the form of larger fees as they gain exposure and establish their reputations.

Earnings

In 1998, median annual earnings for writers were $36,480 a year, according to the *Occupational Outlook Handbook*. The lowest 10 percent earned less than $20,920, while the highest 10 percent earned $76,660. Earnings of those in administrative and supervisory positions are somewhat higher. Experienced writers and researchers are paid $40,000 and over, depending on their qualifications and the size of the publication they work on. In book publishing, some divisions pay better than others.

In addition to their salaries, many writers earn some income from freelance work. Part-time freelancers may earn from $5,000 to $15,000 a year. Freelance earnings vary widely. Full-time established freelance writers may earn up to $75,000 a year.

Work Environment

Working conditions vary for writers. Although the workweek usually runs 35 to 40 hours, many writers work overtime. A publication that is issued frequently has more deadlines closer together, creating greater pressures to meet them. The work is especially hectic on newspapers and at broadcasting companies, which operate seven days a week. Writers often work nights and weekends to meet deadlines or to cover a late-developing story.

Most writers work independently, but they often must cooperate with artists, photographers, rewriters, and advertising people who may have widely differing ideas of how the materials should be prepared and presented.

Physical surroundings range from comfortable private offices to noisy, crowded newsrooms filled with other workers typing and talking on the telephone. Some writers must confine their research to the library or telephone interviews, but others may travel to other cities or countries or to local sites, such as theaters, ballparks, airports, factories, or other offices.

The work is arduous, but writers are seldom bored. Each day brings new and interesting problems. The jobs occasionally require travel. The most difficult element is the continual pressure of deadlines. People who are the most content as writers enjoy and work well with deadline pressure.

Outlook

The employment of writers is expected to increase faster than the average rate of all occupations through 2008. The demand for writers by newspapers, periodicals, book publishers, and nonprofit organizations is expected to increase. Advertising and public relations will also provide job opportunities.

The major book and magazine publishers, broadcasting companies, advertising agencies, public relations firms, and the federal government account for the concentration of writers in large cities such as New York, Chicago, Los Angeles, Boston, Philadelphia, San Francisco, and Washington, DC. Opportunities in small newspapers, corporations, and professional, religious, business, technical, and trade publications can be found throughout the country.

People entering this field should realize that the competition for jobs is extremely keen. Beginners, especially, may have difficulty finding employment. Of the thousands who graduate each year with degrees in English, journalism, communications, and the liberal arts, intending to establish a career as a writer, many turn to other occupations when they find that applicants far outnumber the job openings available. College students would do well to keep this in mind and prepare for an unrelated alternate career in the event they are unable to obtain a position as writer; another benefit of this approach is that, at the same time, they will become qualified as writers in a specialized field. The practicality of preparing for alternate careers is borne out by the fact that opportunities are best in firms that prepare business and trade publications and in technical writing.

Potential writers who end up working in a different field may be able to earn some income as freelancers, selling articles, stories, books, and possibly TV and movie scripts, but it is usually difficult for anyone to be self-supporting entirely on independent writing.

For More Information

Information on writing and editing careers in the field of communications is available from:

National Association of Science Writers
PO Box 294
Greenlawn, NY 11740
Tel: 631-757-5664
Web: http://www.nasw.org/

This organization offers student memberships for those interested in opinion writing.

National Conference of Editorial Writers
6223 Executive Boulevard
Rockville, MD 20852
Tel: 301-984-3015
Email: ncewhqs@erols.com
Web: http://www.ncew.org

Index